TOWARD CLIMATE-RESILIENT ROADS

CLIMATE CHANGE ADAPTATION MEASURES FOR THE ROAD SECTOR IN TIMOR-LESTE

JULY 2024

ASIAN DEVELOPMENT BANK

Corrigenda to ADB publications may be found at http://www.adb.org/publications/corrigenda.

Notes:
In this publication, "$" refers to United States dollars.
ADB recognizes "China" as the People's Republic of China.
The fiscal year (FY) of the government and its agencies ends on 31 December.
Photos are from the study team unless otherwise stated.

Cover design by Mike Cortes.

On the cover: Upper left: A bus at the damaged road section of National Road No. 1 near Baucau.
Upper right: People walking in the flooded section of National Road No. 7 between Viqueque and Natarbora.
Middle right: A rehabilitated road section of National Road No. 3 near Tibar.
Bottom: Engineers inspecting a damaged road section of National Road No. 3 near Maubara.

CONTENTS

TABLES, FIGURES, AND MAPS

MAPS

FOREWORD

Since 2000, the Asian Development Bank (ADB) has been the leading development partner for the road sector in Timor-Leste. With a cumulative funding of approximately $330 million in the sector, ADB has supported the Government of Timor-Leste in rehabilitating and upgrading over 460 kilometers of the road network, mainly covering the northern coast and two north-to-south connections. ADB plans to further extend its support to improve roads in the east and south of the country, aligning with the government's program priorities.

One of the road sector's main challenges is the increasing risk of climate change. Flooding, including both riverine and flash flooding, is the most frequent disaster impacting Timor-Leste, as extreme rainfall events have shown. Cyclone Seroja in April 2021 caused approximately $300 million in damages at an estimated 20% loss of the gross domestic product. Additionally, heavy rains in 2020 and 2021 significantly damaged sections of roads completed with ADB and other donor funding.

Future climate risks are expected to intensify with climate change. Climate models suggest a possible delay in the onset of the rainy season, accompanied by increased rainfall during a condensed period. Moreover, projections indicate further increases in extreme rainfall events toward the end of the century. Thus, infrastructure built over the next decades will operate under vastly different climate conditions compared to today. In other words, climate change will fundamentally alter the framework within which infrastructure—especially infrastructure with longer design life, such as roads—is planned, financed, designed, implemented, and operated.

Understanding climate risk must be a fundamental basis for designing, implementing, and maintaining road infrastructure to ensure that roads continue to provide services and connect remote communities despite increasing climate risks. Improved land use planning, updated construction codes, strengthened budget for operation and maintenance, and improved early warning systems will all be crucial for building road sector resilience.

ADB has committed to becoming "Asia and the Pacific's Climate Bank" and plans to invest $100 billion in climate finance by 2030, doubling its support for climate adaptation. Given Timor-Leste's high vulnerability to climate change, ADB provided technical assistance to assess the climate impact on Timor-Leste's road sector and identify appropriate climate adaptation measures.

The assessment detailed in this report covers 10 road sections and 4 bridges, categorizing the causes of damage. Using global climate change models and local rainfall data, the study assesses and forecasts the impact of climate change in Timor-Leste. It proposes methodologies that national engineers can employ to identify damage causes, emphasizing adaptation measures tailored to the country's specific context rather than offering broad, generalized proposals. Furthermore, the assessment offers strategies for the effective implementation of these measures. These findings need to be reflected in the maintenance and rehabilitation of roadways, as well as the design and construction quality control of new roads.

I am confident that the report's findings will serve as valuable guidance, encouraging collaborative efforts among all stakeholders to advance climate adaptation solutions for the road sector, thereby safeguarding people's lives and livelihoods against the repercussions of climate change.

Stefania Dina
Country Director
Timor-Leste Resident Mission
Asian Development Bank

ACKNOWLEDGMENTS

This report, *Toward Climate-Resilient Roads—Climate Change Adaptation Measures for the Road Sector in Timor-Leste*, was prepared under the technical assistance program of the Asian Development Bank (ADB).

The program and report preparation were led by Takeshi Fukayama, Transport Specialist, Sectors Group, ADB. The team comprised Ronald Mark G. Omaña, Project Analyst, Sectors Group; Pedro Aquino, Senior Project Officer (Infrastructure), Timor-Leste Resident Mission (TLRM); Jose Perreira, Senior Project Officer, TLRM; and Geraldo Moniz Da Silva, Operations Assistant, TLRM. The report's content was prepared by IDEA Consultants, Inc., in collaboration with INGEROSEC Corporation and Kokusai Kogyo Co., Ltd., Japan. From the academic sector, Benjamim Hopffer Martins and Hugo Ximenes, Department of Civil Engineering, Faculty of Engineering, Sciences and Technology, National University of Timor-Leste, contributed to the team and participated in field studies. The report was reviewed by Aruna Nanayakkara, Senior Project Officer (Transport), Sri Lanka Resident Mission; Okju Jeong, Climate Change Specialist, Climate Change and Sustainable Development Department, ADB; and Haiyoung Chang, Technical Advisor under the technical assistance.

The team worked closely with clients in the Government of Timor-Leste, including the Directorate General of Roads, Bridges, Prevention and Flood Control and the Project Management Unit of the Ministry of Public Works. The team assisted government engineers in testing innovative technologies such as a drone equipped with light detection and ranging sensors, satellite-observed rainfall data, and geographic information system mapping for climate adaptation.

To raise public attention about the importance of climate adaptation in the road sector in Timor-Leste, ADB created and disseminated a short video via smart media platforms.

On 24 October 2023, the team hosted a seminar in Dili, Timor-Leste, focusing on climate change adaptation measures for the road sector. The event had over 100 participants representing the Ministry of Public Works, Ministry of Finance, Ministry of Planning and Strategic Investment, Ministry of Tourism and Environment, Authority of Climate Change Adaptation, Embassy of Australia, Embassy of Japan, the World Bank, the United Nations Development Programme, consultants, and civil society organizations. Through presentations and discussions, the seminar played a pivotal role in enhancing the audience's understanding of climate adaptation measures in Timor-Leste's road sector.

I extend my heartfelt gratitude and appreciation to the team for their dedication and effort.

Dong Kyu Lee
Director, Transport Sector Office, Sectors Group
Asian Development Bank

ABBREVIATIONS

ADB	Asian Development Bank
ADN	National Development Agency (Agência de Desenvolvimento Nacional)
AGCM	Atmospheric General Circulation Model
AR6	Sixth Assessment Report
CMIP6	Coupled Model Intercomparison Project Phase 6
DGRBPFC	Directorate General of Roads, Bridges, Prevention and Flood Control
GIS	geographic information system
GSMaP	Global Satellite Mapping of Precipitation
IPCC	Intergovernmental Panel on Climate Change
JAXA	Japan Aerospace Exploration Agency
LiDAR	light detection and ranging
MPW	Ministry of Public Works
MRI	Meteorological Research Institute
RCP	Representative Concentration Pathway

WEIGHTS AND MEASURES

cm	centimeter
km	kilometer
m	meter
m^3	cubic meter
mm	millimeter

EXECUTIVE SUMMARY

Recent historical extreme rainfall events in Timor-Leste have caused extensive damage to road sections, highlighting the critical need to address climate change risks at all stages of road infrastructure development, including design, construction, and maintenance. This study aims to identify the causes of damage to roads and bridges; plan effective climate change adaptation measures; introduce innovative technologies suitable for adaptation; and strengthen the capacity of government engineers to properly oversee the design, construction, and maintenance of road and bridge infrastructures.

This study addresses five fundamental questions:

(1) Why are roads frequently damaged only a few years after construction?

(2) How do we assess and predict the impact of climate change on roads?

(3) How can engineers investigate and identify the cause of damage?

(4) What climate change adaptation measures are appropriate for Timor-Leste?

(5) How can these measures be effectively implemented?

The study assessed the impact of climate change on the road sector in Timor-Leste by using various climate change models and data. By estimating the climate change ratio and future design rainfall, it proposed the applicable box culvert size under historical and future climate scenarios, which can be embedded in the national design standard (**section 2.2**).

The study classified the damages of roads into six cases: (i) landslide, (ii) cut slope failure, (iii) fill slope failure, (iv) settlement, (v) debris flow, and (vi) culvert and ditch. Similarly, it classified the damages to bridges into four cases: (i) inappropriate river cross section, (ii) river course change due to floods, (iii) river course change due to inappropriate installation of revetment walls, and (iv) heavy sedimentation under bridge (**section 2.3**).

For each road damage case, the study identified causes, measurement methods, and countermeasures. For landslides, a comprehensive approach was recommended, using data from satellite imagery, topographic and geological maps, and aerial drone photography. For cut slope failure, the study recommended countermeasures such as rockfall prevention nets and shotcrete. For fill slope failure and settlement, the study identified external factors such as unstable foundations, high rainwater infiltration, erosion during floods, and erosion at the outlet of the culvert. Recommended countermeasures focused on foundation stabilization, introduction of subsoil drain, and appropriate installation of gabion mat. The study also suggested countermeasures for debris flow protection. For culverts and ditches, it recommended performing flow calculations in response to climate change, designing culvert inlets and outlets to absorb rainfall and rainfall pressure, and incorporating maintenance considerations. Additionally, the study introduced community-based climate adaptation measures such as bioengineering solutions with community participation (**section 2.4**).

In the case of bridge damage, the study identified causes and countermeasures from both structural and river engineering perspectives. It proposed installing a relief open bridge, planting trees, conducting rooting works around the piers, and installing groins to protect the riverbank gabion wall. In response to heavy sedimentation under the bridge and changes in the river course, it suggested alternative bypass routes based on flood simulation analysis (**section 2.5**).

Under the study, field workshops and technical training were conducted for government staff to observe road damages, receive technical briefings, and test innovative technologies such as a light detection and ranging drone, satellite-observed rainfall data, and geographic information system mapping for climate adaptation (**section 2.6**).

Lastly, the study identified the following key points for future road development (**section 3**):

- Climate adaptation measures are essential throughout **all project cycles, including design, construction, and maintenance**.
- The implementing agency, serving as **the Employer, should be empowered** to manage climate resilience by adopting technical standards and unified guidelines that are responsive to climate changes.
- **A comprehensive approach** is recommended for technical assessments, encouraging engineers to conduct these from broader perspectives and using various data sources.
- **A risk-based approach** is suggested for selecting climate adaptation measures, based on cost–benefit analysis to ensure alignment with the local context and available technologies.
- **Community participation and perception** are crucial for effective climate adaptation.

1 INTRODUCTION

Recent historical extreme rainfall events in Timor-Leste have highlighted the urgent need to integrate climate change risk management throughout the design, construction, and maintenance phases of road infrastructure. In 2020 and 2021, heavy rains resulted in settlements, landslides, washouts of road sections, and damage to bridges on projects funded by the Asian Development Bank (ADB) and other donors. Diagnoses of the causes of these issues and proposals for climate change adaptation measures are required to be embedded in the engineering design of future road projects in Timor-Leste, including the East to South Coast Road Connectivity Project, as well as in community participation programs. Additionally, enhancing the capacity of government staff and stakeholders through knowledge dissemination on climate change adaptation measures is critical.

To improve the effectiveness of its assistance, ADB classifies Timor-Leste as a country in fragile and conflict-affected situations and as a small island developing state. At the 56th ADB Annual Meeting in Incheon, ADB announced plans to significantly boost support for the region in combating climate change, positioning itself as the climate bank for Asia and the Pacific. ADB's country partnership strategy for Timor-Leste for 2023–2027 is designed to aid the country's economic recovery, inclusive development, and climate-resilience efforts, including improving the quality of infrastructure governance and public investment management.

The Government of Timor-Leste has updated and expanded its Nationally Determined Contribution (2022–2030) to the United Nations Framework Convention on Climate Change Paris Agreement, building on its initial Nationally Determined Contribution (2016). This revision emphasizes the country's commitment to incorporating climate risk management across all sectoral policies, planning processes, implementation strategies, and investments. Central to this effort is the National Climate Change Policy (2021), which serves as the primary policy framework for guiding Timor-Leste's climate change strategy. This policy introduces a commitment to developing a Climate Change Law, establishing a legal framework for the country's climate change response.

Consistent with these policies, a study was conducted to identify the causes of damage to roads and bridges; devise effective climate change adaptation measures; implement innovative technologies for climate adaptation; and strengthen the capacity of government engineers to properly oversee and manage the design, construction, and maintenance of road and bridge infrastructures.[1] This knowledge product summarizes the study's findings.

---

[1]   ADB. 2021. *Technical Assistance to Timor-Leste for Preparing the East to South Coast Road Connectivity Project and Strengthening the Road Sector Institutional Capacity.*

2 CLIMATE CHANGE ADAPTATION MEASURES FOR THE ROAD SECTOR IN TIMOR-LESTE

2.1 | Outline of the Road Sector in Timor-Leste

Transport is crucial in supporting a "modern and productive country in which its people are connected with each other and with the world," as recognized by the Government of Timor-Leste's Strategic Development Plan, 2011–2030.[2] Road transport accounts for about 90% of passenger and 70% of freight movement in the country. With an estimated 70% of the population living in rural areas, improving the core road network that links municipalities and provides access to villages and remote areas is vital for local socioeconomic development. Upgrading road transport will boost productivity in agriculture, industry, and tourism, aiding in economic diversification. Timor-Leste boasts a road network of about 7,500 kilometers (km), of which 4,700 km are rural roads. About 1,400 km of national roads connect the capital, Dili, with the 12 municipalities, while 770 km of municipal roads link major population centers to national roads.[3] Despite significant investments from development partners in rehabilitating, upgrading, and improving roads, there is still a need to enhance road network connectivity. The vehicle fleet in Timor-Leste expanded rapidly during 2015–2019, with an average increase of 2.3% in new vehicle registrations annually, including an 8.0% increase in motorbikes. Map 1 shows the national roads in Timor-Leste and the funding sources for road improvement.

Timor-Leste is among the countries most vulnerable to climate variability and change because of its location, mountainous topography, and exposure to hydrometeorological influences and extreme climate events. The country faces heightened risks of landslides, road settlements, severe flooding, and erosion and sedimentation resulting from increasingly frequent extreme rainfall events affecting inland roads. Coastal roads are also at risk of flooding and inundation from the combined impacts of cyclones, storm surges, and sea-level rise. The photos on p. 3 depict typical damages to roads and bridges caused by recent severe rainfall events.

---

[2]   Government of Timor-Leste. 2011. *Timor-Leste Strategic Development Plan, 2011–2030*. p. 70.

[3]   ADB. 2019. *Baucau to Viqueque Highway Project: Technical Assistance Consultant's Report*.

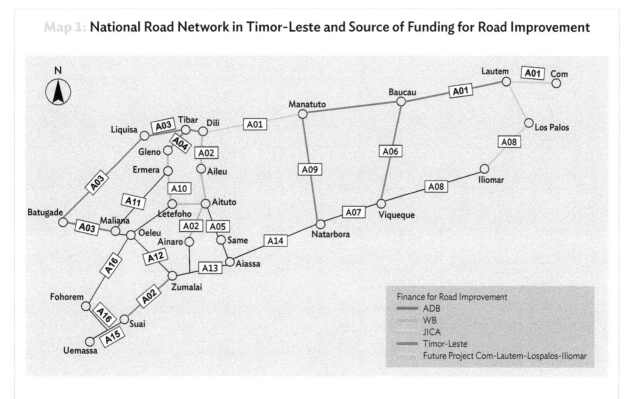

Map 1: **National Road Network in Timor-Leste and Source of Funding for Road Improvement**

ADB = Asian Development Bank, JICA = Japan International Cooperation Agency, WB = World Bank.
Source: Study team.

Road Damage

Landslide. Landslides, with a movement of soils in larger areas, have caused cracking, settlement, and lateral movement of the road surface, highlighting the ongoing risks and the critical need for durable infrastructure.

Cut slope failure. Debris from an unstable hillside cut slope obstructs the road, while a heavy equipment removes the debris from the road. It is important to set cut slopes that match the soil conditions of the slope and the surrounding topography.

Fill slope failure. A construction road on steeply sloping land is compromised by the downward movement of an engineered embankment, highlighting the importance of robust earthworks and drainage design.

Settlement. Flooding from the river in the valley and water seeping under the embankment from the mountainside have caused the road to lose its bearing capacity and settle massively.

Debris flow. Stones and sand carried by debris flows are deposited in front of the box culvert, reducing the water flow area. It is important to remove the stones and sand urgently to open the culvert.

Culvert and ditch failure. Erosion and structural damage around a drainage culvert disrupt the adjacent road, highlighting maintenance and design challenges.

Bridge Damage

Scouring of abutment foundation. Erosion at the foundations exposes and weakens the bridge's critical support, underscoring erosion's threat to structural integrity.

Bridge approach washed out. The access road to the bridge has been lost and is completely inoperative.

Massive sediment deposits under the bridge. A bridge overshadowed by significant sediment deposits underneath, affecting its stability and water flow.

This study examines climate adaptation measures for Timor-Leste's national road network, which underwent rehabilitation financed by ADB. Certain sections of this network sustained damage from recent severe rains, necessitating the implementation of such measures.

In addressing critical concerns, the study explores five fundamental questions:

(1) Why are roads frequently damaged only a few years after construction?

(2) How do we assess and predict the impact of climate change on roads?

(3) How can engineers investigate and identify the cause of the damage?

(4) What climate change adaptation measures are appropriate for Timor-Leste?

(5) How can these measures be effectively implemented?

2.2 | Impact of Climate Change on the Road Sector in Timor-Leste

Global Climate Change

According to the Sixth Assessment Report (AR6) of the Intergovernmental Panel on Climate Change (IPCC), the global average surface temperature during 2011–2020 was 1.1°C higher relative to 1850–1890 (Figure 1). To meet the Paris Agreement targets, governments must ensure that the rise in global surface temperature remains below 0.9°C and, if possible, below 0.4°C in the future.

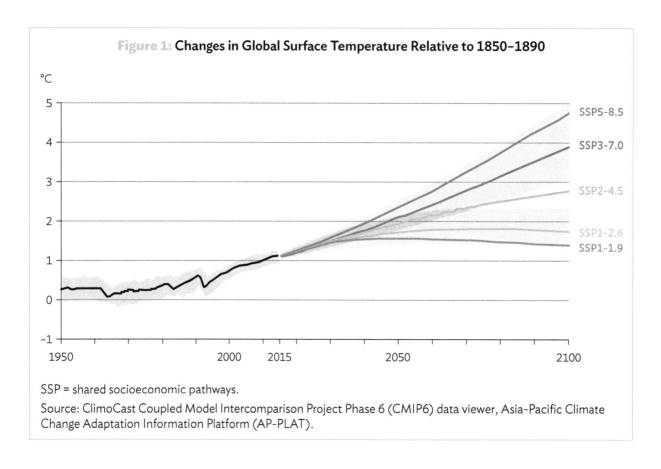

Figure 1: Changes in Global Surface Temperature Relative to 1850–1890

SSP = shared socioeconomic pathways.
Source: ClimoCast Coupled Model Intercomparison Project Phase 6 (CMIP6) data viewer, Asia-Pacific Climate Change Adaptation Information Platform (AP-PLAT).

Figure 2 illustrates the anticipated future changes in surface air temperature in Timor-Leste, as projected by 10 representative global climate models in the Coupled Model Intercomparison Project Phase 6 (CMIP6).[4] The projections are based on four shared socioeconomic pathways scenarios and are presented as differences from the 1981–2000 average.

While the degree of temperature increase varies depending on the shared socioeconomic pathways scenario, temperatures in Timor-Leste are predicted to rise by about 0.5°C–6.0°C by the end of the 21st century.

---

4   Details can be found on Asia-Pacific Climate Adaptation Infrastructure Platform. https://a-plat.nies.go.jp/ap-plat/cmip6/global.html.

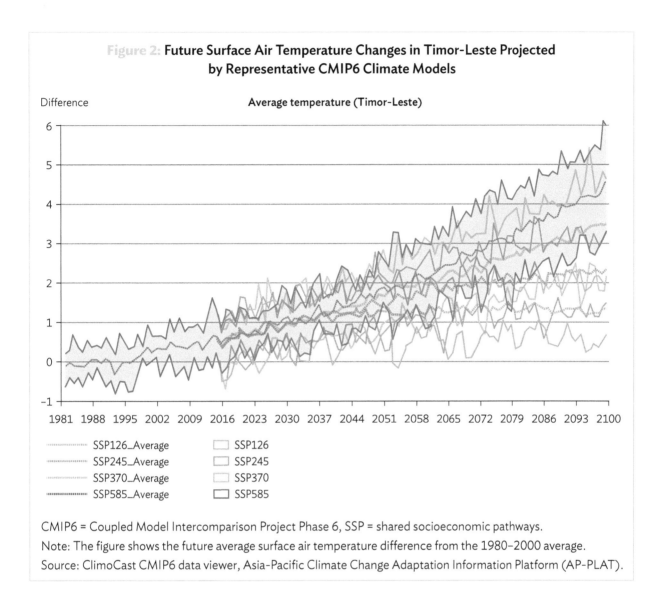

Figure 2: Future Surface Air Temperature Changes in Timor-Leste Projected by Representative CMIP6 Climate Models

CMIP6 = Coupled Model Intercomparison Project Phase 6, SSP = shared socioeconomic pathways.

Note: The figure shows the future average surface air temperature difference from the 1980–2000 average.

Source: ClimoCast CMIP6 data viewer, Asia-Pacific Climate Change Adaptation Information Platform (AP-PLAT).

Global warming is expected to increase the frequency of localized torrential downpours and, conversely, periods of no rainfall.

According to the IPCC AR6 Working Group 1 Interactive Atlas, heavy precipitation and pluvial flooding in Timor-Leste are projected to increase with high confidence (Figure 3).

However, evaluating extreme events quantitatively using global climate models is challenging due to their coarse resolution (about 1 degree x 1 degree). High-resolution data are crucial for detailed analysis of these extreme events. Additionally, it is necessary to consider extreme events on shorter timescales than those usually used in engineering design studies. Projects such as World Climate Research Programme, Coordinated Regional Climate Downscaling Experiment are generating regionally downscaled data. This information is needed to quantitatively consider the impact of climate change on engineering design.

Figure 3: Evaluation of Future Heavy Precipitation and Pluvial Flood around Timor-Leste

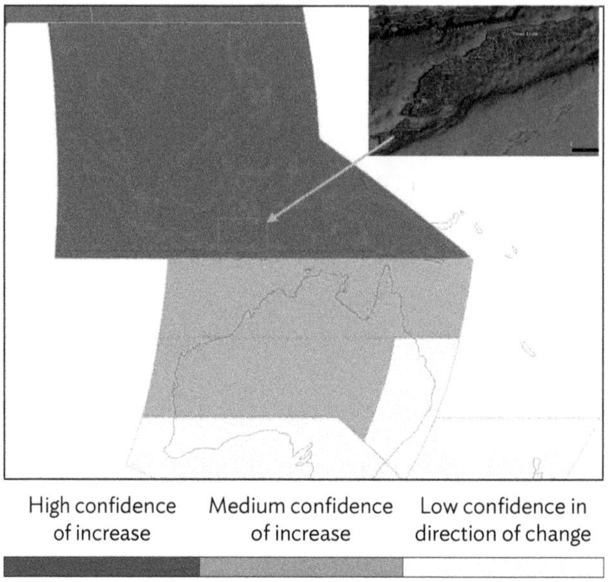

| High confidence of increase | Medium confidence of increase | Low confidence in direction of change |

Map data: Google, Data Scripps Institution of Oceanography (SIO), National Oceanic and Atmospheric Administration (NOAA), United States (US) Navy, National Geospatial-Intelligence Agency (NGA), General Bathymetric Chart of the Oceans (GEBCO), Image © Landsat/Copernicus.

Source: Intergovernmental Panel on Climate Change (IPCC) Sixth Assessment Report (AR6) Working Group 1 Interactive Atlas: Regional Synthesis.

Methodology to Quantitatively Evaluate the Impact of Climate Change

Several examples demonstrate the quantification of climate change impacts from high-resolution modeling results. Climate change allowances, quantifying future changes in rainfall and flow rates, are employed in flood countermeasure studies in several countries.

In Japan, the climate change ratio, which compares future and historical rainfall, informs river management plans and rainwater drainage systems, as depicted in Table 1.

Using the Japanese method, the study team estimated Timor-Leste's climate change ratio from four historical or Representative Concentration Pathway 2.6 (RCP2.6) scenario[5] patterns of the Meteorological Research Institute Atmospheric General Circulation Model version 20 (MRI-AGCM20),[6] the highest-resolution global climate model known to cover Timor-Leste.

---

[5]   In the RCP2.6 scenario, the global average temperature at the end of the 21st century (2081–2100) is likely to rise by 0.9°C–2.3°C compared to pre-industrial levels. This range corresponds to the climate outcomes anticipated by the Paris Agreement's goal of limiting global warming to 2°C. Therefore, in this report, the RCP2.6 scenario is equated with a +2°C. While datasets for RCP8.5 scenarios are also available, this report exclusively discusses the results for RCP2.6 (+2°C), assuming the Paris Agreement's targets are met.

[6]   Data Integration and Analysis System. Climate Projection Data with 20km-Mesh AGCM by SOUSEI Program. https://search.diasjp.net/en/dataset/GCM20_SOUSEI.

Table 1: **Climate Change Ratio Set for Each Area of River Management as Used in Japan**

Future Climate Change Ratios for Flooding			
Scenario	Rainfall	Discharge	Flooding Frequency
+2°C	1.1	1.2	2.0
+4°C	1.3	1.4	4.0
Climate Change Ratios by Region for Rainfall			
Region/Scenario	+2°C	+4°C[a]	
North	1.15	1.4–1.5	
West	1.1	1.4–1.5	
Others	1.1	1.2–1.3	

Future design rainfall = Historical design rainfall x ratio

[a] The ratio varies depending on the timescale of rainfall.

Source: Government of Japan, Ministry of Land, Infrastructure, Transport and Tourism.

For historical design rainfall, the study team used location-based rainfall data from Global Satellite Mapping of Precipitation (GSMaP),[7] which has over 25 years of data at hourly intervals since 1998 and shows a similar trend of change to rain-gauge data. This approach was necessary because rain-gauge stations in Timor-Leste are sparse, and rain-gauge data are stored for only the most recent 15 years at daily intervals in almost all locations.

Using these data, the study team estimated the climate change ratio and future design rainfall, then introduced the concept of engineering design considering future climate change.

Engineering Design Considering Future Climate Change

In 2022, the Directorate General of Roads, Bridges, Prevention and Flood Control (DGRBPFC) within Timor-Leste's Ministry of Public Works (MPW) developed the *Guidelines for Road Drainage—Culvert Design*. In this part, the study team introduces how to apply the climate change ratio to culvert design as a case study based on the guidelines, using the Lospalos–Iliomar section of National Road A08, which is part of the East to South Coast Road Connectivity Project. Specifically, the results for the Iliomar area are detailed. Since the focus is on national highways, the study examines the historical/future 10-year return period of rainfall. The point where the road and watercourse intersect is defined as the culvert location. In the Iliomar area, the study team identified 25 sites that need culverts and applied the rational method to design these culverts' flood capacity according to the guidelines.

---

[7] JAXA Global Rainfall Watch. https://sharaku.eorc.jaxa.jp/GSMaP/guide.html.

Historical Design Rainfall

Based on the method described in the guidelines, historical design rainfall around Iliomar is set at 84 millimeters (mm) per hour (Figure 4). The study team evaluated the applicable box culvert size by computing the design flood for 25 catchment areas of culvert for historical climate around Iliomar.

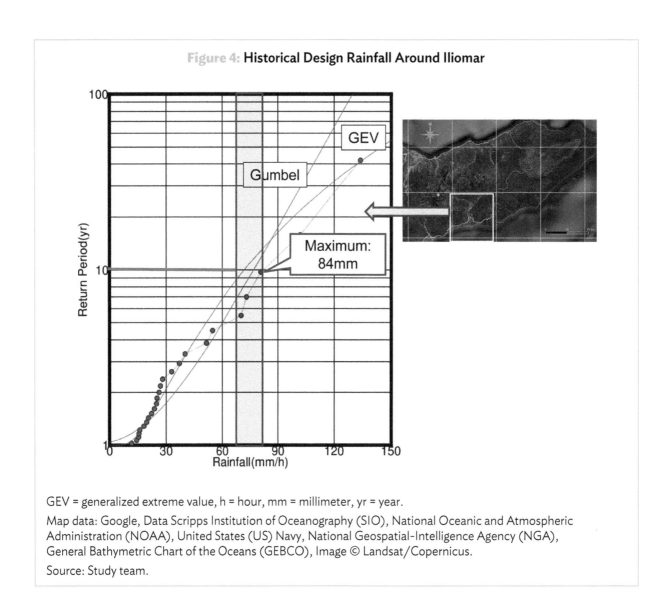

Figure 4: **Historical Design Rainfall Around Iliomar**

GEV = generalized extreme value, h = hour, mm = millimeter, yr = year.

Map data: Google, Data Scripps Institution of Oceanography (SIO), National Oceanic and Atmospheric Administration (NOAA), United States (US) Navy, National Geospatial-Intelligence Agency (NGA), General Bathymetric Chart of the Oceans (GEBCO), Image © Landsat/Copernicus.

Source: Study team.

Climate Change Ratios

The climate change ratios ranged from 0.7 to 2.0 across four patterns. The mechanisms are complex, with El Niño conditions leading to fewer instances of heavy rainfall and La Niña conditions resulting in more instances of heavy rainfall.

For simplicity, the dataset integrating all four patterns was considered the most reliable due to its large sample size. This assumption led to a calculated ratio of 1.4. With this ratio, future design rainfall was calculated to be 118 mm/hour (84 mm x 1.4), as shown in Figure 5.

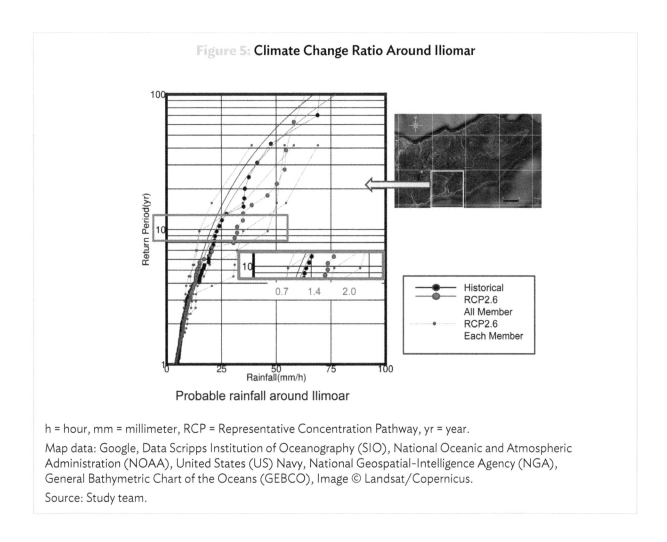

Figure 5: Climate Change Ratio Around Iliomar

Probable rainfall around Ilimoar

h = hour, mm = millimeter, RCP = Representative Concentration Pathway, yr = year.

Map data: Google, Data Scripps Institution of Oceanography (SIO), National Oceanic and Atmospheric Administration (NOAA), United States (US) Navy, National Geospatial-Intelligence Agency (NGA), General Bathymetric Chart of the Oceans (GEBCO), Image © Landsat/Copernicus.

Source: Study team.

Evaluation of Applicable Box Culvert Size Under Historical and Future Climate Scenarios

The calculated rainfall data were used to determine the design flood, which was then compared with the design capacity of each box culvert size to select the applicable size for each location. Culvert sizes for historical climate rainfall are shown on the left side of Figure 6, while those for future climate rainfall appear on the right side. The study found that, around Iliomar, one out of 25 culverts needs resizing to accommodate future rainfall projections.

Direction for Engineering Design of Culverts Considering Future Climate Conditions

Design Rainfall to Be Considered in Engineering Design

The study concludes that

- rainfall characteristics vary by location, necessitating the use of location-based rainfall data in engineering design; and

- engineering design should incorporate adaptation measures for both historical and future climate conditions.

Figure 6: Applicable Culvert Size Recommended for Future Climate Around Iliomar

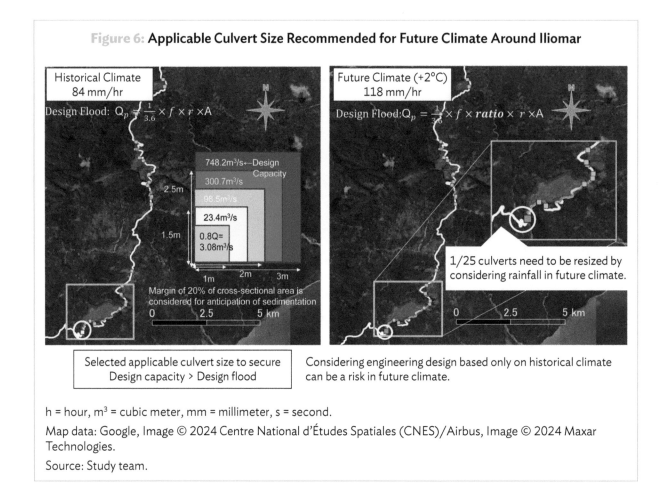

Selected applicable culvert size to secure Design capacity > Design flood

Considering engineering design based only on historical climate can be a risk in future climate.

h = hour, m³ = cubic meter, mm = millimeter, s = second.

Map data: Google, Image © 2024 Centre National d'Études Spatiales (CNES)/Airbus, Image © 2024 Maxar Technologies.

Source: Study team.

Recommended Climate Change Ratio Around National Road A08 (Iliomar–Lospalos) at +2°C

Based on this study's assessment, the climate change ratio around National Road A08 (Iliomar–Lospalos) is detailed in Table 2. The ratio for short-term rainfall is generally higher, which is consistent with the general perspective that short-term rainfall will be more intense due to global warming.

Table 2: Climate Change Ratio Around National Road A08 (Iliomar–Lospalos)

Hydrological Factor	1 hour	3 hours–12 hours	Daily
Rainfall	1.4	1.1–1.2	1.1
Discharge (small catchment area)	1.4	…	…
Discharge (> = 15 km² catchment area)	…	…	1.2
River velocity	…	…	1.1
Water level (depth)	…	…	1.1

km² = square kilometer.

Source: Study team.

2.3 | Classification of Road and Bridge Damage

The previous chapter discussed the impact of climate change in Timor-Leste and recommended the climate change ratio for specific road sections, using analysis from MRI-AGCM20, a high-resolution global climate change model, and GSMaP, a rainfall dataset that accurately expresses regional historical rainfall characteristics.

This chapter categorizes the damage to roads and bridges to clearly understand the causes and identify appropriate adaptation measures.

Roads

Analysis of road section damage resulting from recent extreme rainfall events was conducted on 10 road cases among the projects funded by ADB and other donors. The damage observed in Timor-Leste's road infrastructure falls into three main categories: (i) landslide and slope collapse, (ii) damaged surfaces, and (iii) damaged drainage facilities (Figure 7). The categories of landslide and slope collapse are further divided into landslide and cut slope failure. Damaged surfaces are categorized into fill slope failure and settlement. Lastly, damaged drainage facilities are classified into debris flow, and culvert and ditch.

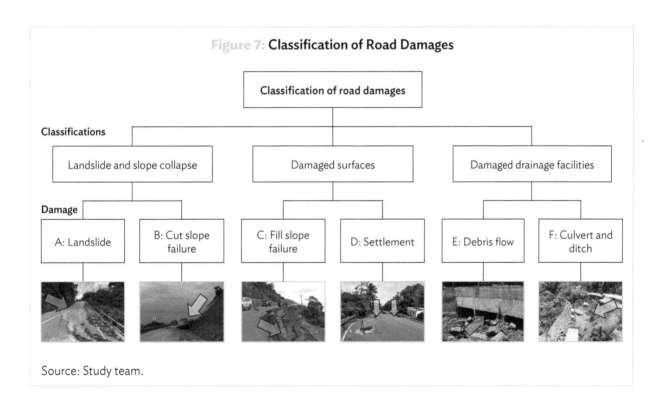

Figure 7: Classification of Road Damages

Source: Study team.

Bridges

Four target bridges were analyzed for damage in the study: Loes, Dilor, Welolo, and Irabere. The bridges were classified into two major damage types: bridge approach washed out and heavy sedimentation under the bridge.

The damage type "bridge approach washed out" can be classified into three subtypes of damage: inappropriate river cross section (Loes Bridge), river course change due to floods (Dilor Bridge), and river course change due to the inappropriate installation of revetment walls (Irabere Bridge) (Figure 8).

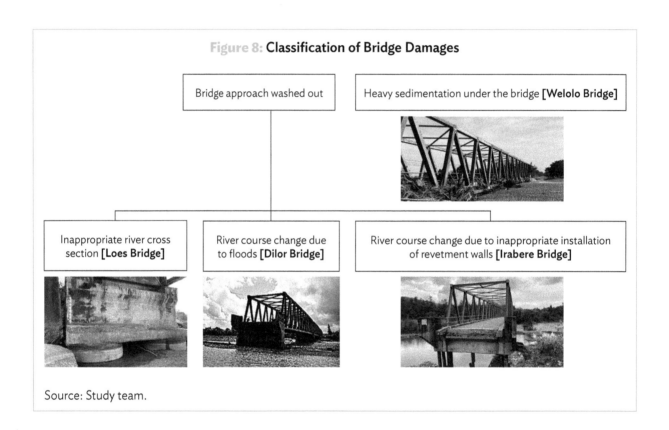

Figure 8: **Classification of Bridge Damages**

Bridge approach washed out

Heavy sedimentation under the bridge **[Welolo Bridge]**

Inappropriate river cross section **[Loes Bridge]**

River course change due to floods **[Dilor Bridge]**

River course change due to inappropriate installation of revetment walls **[Irabere Bridge]**

Source: Study team.

2.4 | Road Damage and Countermeasures

The previous section introduced the classification of road and bridge damage caused by recent historical severe rains in Timor-Leste. This section discusses how engineers investigate damage causes and what climate adaptation measures would be effective for each classified road damage.

Landslide

The study team took a comprehensive approach to the problem of damaged road embankments, obtaining ideas for countermeasures (Figure 9). Data collection, on-site inspection, analysis, and hypothesis building were conducted. Subsurface information from ground investigations revealed the spatial extent of the problem. Countermeasures were devised based on the investigation results, and a plan was formulated to manipulate natural conditions and introduce artificial structures.

Figure 9: **Comprehensive Approach to Landslides**

Road damages	Approach	Outcome
	1. Desktop study	1. Background, analyze, hypothesis
	2. Site reconnaissance	2. Natural condition, prediction
	3. Investigation	3. Facts on site, understanding the structure of problems
	4. Design and planning	4. Estimation, envision for countermeasures
	5. Implementation	5. Safety traffic for road users

Source: Study team.

Information gathering and field surveys included data from satellite imagery, topographic and geological maps, and aerial drone photography. Underground investigations such as ground-penetrating radar, electrical exploration, and borehole drilling (N-value indexed by standard penetration tests and groundwater surveys) determined the subsurface extent of the landslide. The study team then assessed how the landslide impacted the road by reversing the road construction process in the landslide area. Stability calculations confirmed that road embankment failure leads to a rapid decrease in effective stress due to groundwater rise, sharply reducing the safety factor (Figure 10).[8]

The design and construction plan for countermeasures reviewed the failure mechanism, proposing two types: (i) measures to restore the safety factor by removing the main factors (natural conditions) that led to the collapse (control works), and (ii) measures to increase the safety factor with artificial structures like reinforced concrete (restrain works). The cost of each measure was estimated.

For roads in mountainous or hilly areas, potentially within landslide zones, using satellite information, topographic maps, and aerial photography via geographic information system (GIS) is crucial for identifying the extent of potential landslide areas. Road construction should include (i) measures to prevent road alignment from entering the landslide area; and (ii) measures to mitigate landslide effects, if the road alignment cannot avoid the landslide area.

---

8   The safety factor of a slope is the ratio of resistance forces to sliding forces. If the safety factor is less than or equal to 1, the slope will fail as sliding forces will equal or exceed the resistance forces. A safety factor significantly greater than 1 indicates a stable slope.

Figure 10: Example of a Comprehensive Approach to Landslide

1. Desktop Study

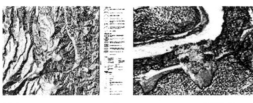

Utilization of maps, satellite imaginaries, and GIS data

2. Site Reconnaissance

Checking cracks/site reconnaissance

3. Investigation

Drilling boring/inclinometer to grasp the slip surface

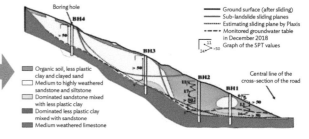

Preparation of cross-section drawings based on the investigation results

4. Planning and Design

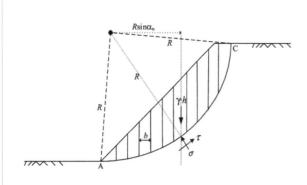

Analyses of the slope stability

Planning and design of countermeasures such as lateral boring works, anchor works, etc.

5. Implementation

Gabion walls

Ground anchor

Drainage boring

Concrete frame

Increase Safety Factor (Fs) to 1.2–1.5
Fs = Resistance force/Sliding force

Source: Study team.

When planning road layouts, conducting topographic and geological surveys over a larger area than merely the specific road section is advisable to help predict post-construction risks. Countermeasures should be aligned with the severity of risks, leading to risk management decisions—whether risks are acceptable, avoidable, or relocatable. Early in the planning process, understanding the uncertainties related to natural conditions is crucial for the development of road infrastructure.

Cut Slope Failure

To maintain and manage road slopes on national roads, the Ministry of Land, Infrastructure, Transport and Tourism in Japan uses the "Slope Stability Survey for Road Slope Inspection" method (Figure 11).

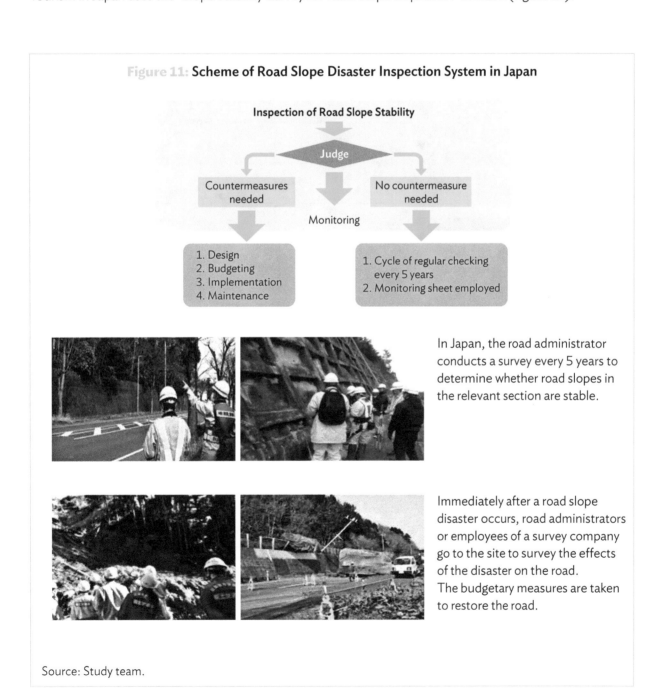

Figure 11: Scheme of Road Slope Disaster Inspection System in Japan

In Japan, the road administrator conducts a survey every 5 years to determine whether road slopes in the relevant section are stable.

Immediately after a road slope disaster occurs, road administrators or employees of a survey company go to the site to survey the effects of the disaster on the road. The budgetary measures are taken to restore the road.

Source: Study team.

The study team applied this method to two slopes on National Road A03 and two slopes on National Road A09. A survey form (General Information Sheet) is used for the survey as presented in Figure 12. The survey results were used in the design and estimation of road disaster prevention measures in this study.

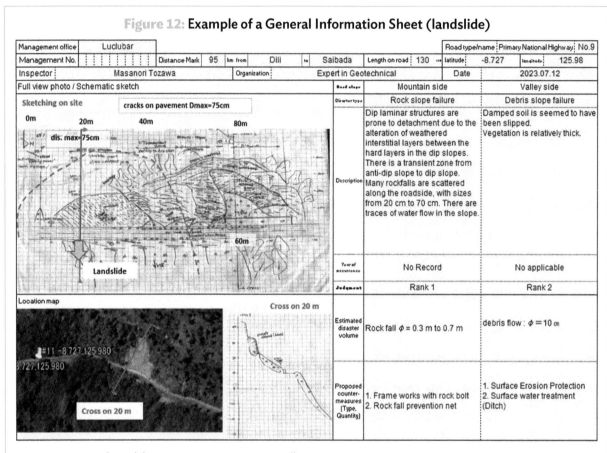

Figure 12: Example of a General Information Sheet (landslide)

cm = centimeter, km = kilometer, m = meter, mm = millimeter.
Source: Study team.

Specifically, on National Road A03, a metamorphic rock slope mainly consisting of pelitic schist was observed. The rocks in the analyzed section had become brittle due to weathering (oxidation) along the schist structure, causing rockfalls and landslides. On National Road A09, a significant landslide at the mountaintop where the road extends caused large cracks and deformation. The metamorphic rock slope had become brittle due to weathering, leading to a cliff collapse and the accumulation of falling rocks and sediment on the road, obstructing traffic.

The Slope Stability Study for Road Slope Inspection method classifies disasters into landslides, slope failure, and rockfalls, extracting the topographic and geological elements that constitute each disaster (hazard). A quantitative evaluation was conducted based on each element's collapse risk, and priorities for countermeasures post-disaster were identified.

For the two slopes on National Road A03, shotcrete with formwork and gutters is recommended to exclude surface water; for National Road A09, landslide countermeasures, sprayed formwork, and gutters are also recommended to exclude surface water.

Timor-Leste's road network, traversing steeply terraced coastal areas and the island's spine, sometimes requires cutting the mountainside and filling the valley side with cut sediment to maintain road width. Topographic and geological conditions (weathering, alteration, erosion, inflow of surface water and groundwater, possible rockfalls, and steep cliffs) must be carefully checked, with countermeasures considered from the planning stage. Depending on the disaster type, an economic risk assessment in road maintenance is essential for ensuring safety and decision-making. Potential damages for economic assessment include loss of life and vehicle damage from landslides, cut slope failure, falling rocks, logistics delays, and time loss due to road slope disasters.

Rockfall prevention net. High-strength nets and flexible wire ropes contour to the terrain, stabilizing even the most irregular slopes (photo from Tokyo Rope).

Rockfall protection net. Designed with durable materials, these nets effectively catch and guide falling rocks to the slope's base, simplifying cleanup and enhancing road safety (photo from Tokyo Rope).

Shotcrete. Enhancing slope stability with a durable mix, this fiber-reinforced shotcrete adheres to complex surfaces, offering long-term protection against erosion and rockfalls (photo from ABC Polymer Industries).

Shotcrete with formwork. Skilled workers apply advanced shotcrete techniques, reinforcing slopes with precision and care to prevent erosion and ensure safety (photo from Nittoc Construction).

Fill Slope Failure and Settlement

Damage

The assessment of road damage due to fill slope failures and settlements has been conducted. Table 3 shows that most road damages are attributed to external factors.

Table 3: External Factors Influencing Fill Slope Failures and Settlements

No.	External Factors	Fill Slope Failures	Settlements
1	Cases with unstable fill foundations, such as grounds with low-bearing capacity	Applicable	Applicable
2	Cases of instability, such as fills on steeply sloping land	Applicable	Applicable
3	Cases of high rainwater infiltration into the fill's interior	Applicable	Applicable
4	Erosion of the slope rim during floods (fills in ponds, along valleys)	Applicable	Applicable
5	Erosion at the culvert's outlet side due to hydraulic pressure	Applicable	—
6	Water entering the fill's interior due to a damaged culvert	—	Applicable

Source: Study team.

The road damage related to an unstable fill foundation (Table 3, factor 1) and instability (Table 3, factor 2) was analyzed. The causes of damage include the foundation's insufficient bearing capacity and the circular slide of the road shoulder due to fill on a steep slope (Figure 13). For this cut and fill section, a subsoil drain is recommended at the boundary between the cut and fill, especially if pore pressure is very high during the rainy season. Furthermore, if the valley side features a retaining wall, installing weep holes is crucial.

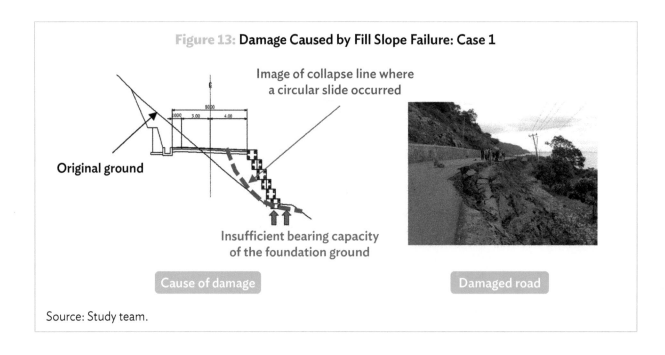

Figure 13: Damage Caused by Fill Slope Failure: Case 1

Image of collapse line where a circular slide occurred

Original ground

Insufficient bearing capacity of the foundation ground

Cause of damage

Damaged road

Source: Study team.

The analysis also covered road damage due to an unstable fill foundation (Table 3, factor 1) and erosion at the culvert's outlet side by hydraulic pressure (Table 3, factor 5). The existing retaining wall and culvert collapsed due to the foundation ground's lack of bearing capacity (Figure 14).

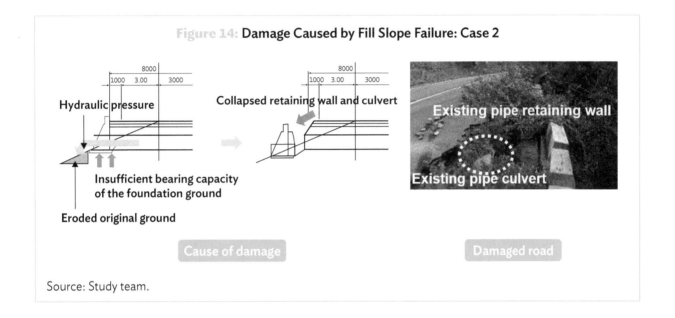

Figure 14: **Damage Caused by Fill Slope Failure: Case 2**

Source: Study team.

The road damage was attributed to external factors no. 1 and no. 4 in Table 3. The shoulder side of the damaged area is affected by the confluence of two valleys, where it was determined that the gabion mat collapsed due to water pressure from the merging valleys (Figure 15).

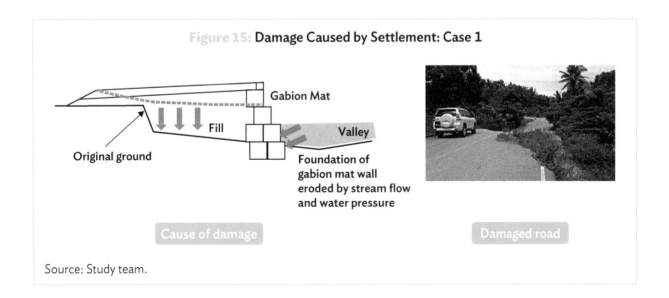

Figure 15: **Damage Caused by Settlement: Case 1**

Source: Study team.

The analysis of road damage considered the influence of external factors no. 3 and no. 5, as indicated in Table 3. Road damage resulted from two main causes. Firstly, the stream's topography allowed rainfall to infiltrate the fill, weakening the soil's bearing capacity at the boundary between the fill and the original ground. Secondly, water pressure created a gap at the junction between the culvert and the inlet wall (Figure 16).

Figure 16: **Damage Situation of Settlement: Case 2**

Source: Study team.

Countermeasures

To address fill slope failure and settlement as climate change adaptation measures, the study team proposes strategies to avoid the external factors listed in Table 3.

For unstable fill foundations, such as low-bearing capacity ground

In cases of unstable foundations, the bearing capacity of the foundation ground under the fill and any structures built at the fill's edge (such as retaining walls, gabion mats, etc.) should be assessed. Even if the design confirms sufficient bearing capacity, verifying it on-site before construction is crucial. Methods for assessing bearing capacity include core boreholes (standard penetration test), plate loading tests, and dynamic cone penetration tests.

If the foundation's bearing capacity is insufficient, two reinforcing methods are suggested: (i) replacing the low-bearing capacity ground with high-quality material, or (ii) improving the ground with cement.

Instability, such as fills on steeply sloping land

For road widening with additional fill, it is preferable to construct the new fill by bench-cutting the existing fill slope, as shown in Figure 17(a).

There are many examples of fill failure from rain or earthquakes on inclined grounds with added narrow fills. Securing slope stability requires more cutting, as Figure 17(b) illustrates. Ideally, the bottom of cut slopes should be horizontal for additional fill. Subsoil drains (filter drains) significantly help maintain the ground's bearing capacity and should be installed at the boundary between cut and fill. Furthermore, the flexibility to add subsoil drains during construction can enhance long-term stability for widened fill areas.

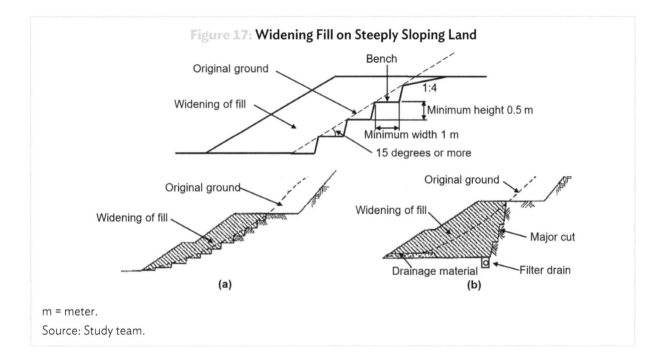

Figure 17: **Widening Fill on Steeply Sloping Land**

m = meter.
Source: Study team.

High rainwater infiltration into the interior of the fill
(spring water from the ground and fill in a valley)

When a fill is placed in a valley and encounters spring water, a drainage layer should be installed at the boundary between the fill and the ground to prevent water retention, as shown in Figure 18. The design should be based on the placement of permeable gravel of 30–50 centimeters (cm) depth as a drainage material or filter drain, including a slotted pipe.

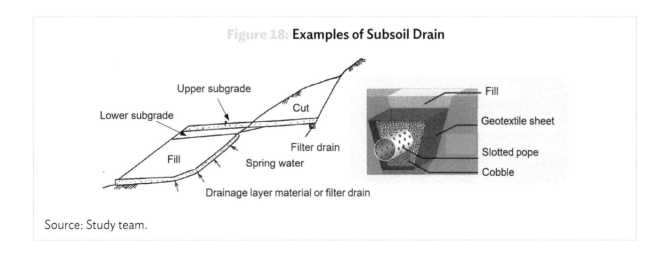

Figure 18: **Examples of Subsoil Drain**

Source: Study team.

Erosion of the slope rim during floods (fills in ponds, along valley)

In Timor-Leste, fills constructed along valleys and streams are reinforced at the base with gabion mats. These mats should be made of materials resistant to erosion from water volume and pressure, and should rest on a foundation with an embedment length of 50–100 cm. Gabion mats should also be piled to specifications, with the backside mechanically compacted for stability (Figure 19).

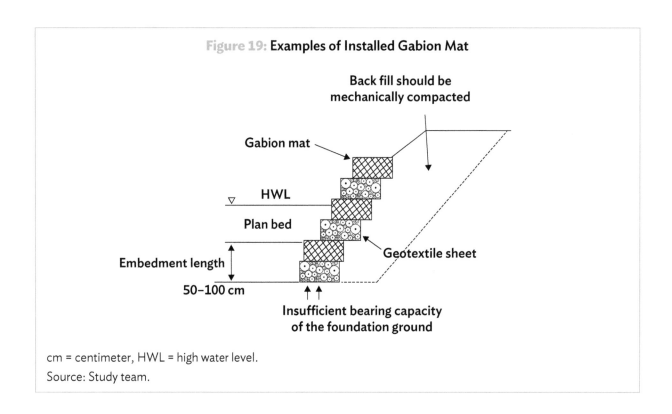

Figure 19: Examples of Installed Gabion Mat

cm = centimeter, HWL = high water level.
Source: Study team.

Erosion at the culvert's outlet side due to hydraulic pressure and water infiltration into the fill from a damaged culvert

This issue is detailed in the section "Designing culvert inlets and outlets to manage rainfall and rainfall pressure" under "Culvert and Ditch" on pp. 25–26.

Debris Flow

Damage

Three box culverts at this location were blocked with rock and soil debris on the upstream side, leading to a significant reduction of their capacity to convey floodwater. The dimensions of the box culverts, measured from the downstream side, are 3 meters (m) x 3 m, with their capacity reduced by up to 75%. The downstream side features stair stepping to slow the flow velocity. Upstream, no debris flow protection measures have been implemented, and the box culvert has a reduced cross section for water flow due to sediment and rock accumulation.

The box culvert is prone to blockage and could damage the road, especially on the upstream side, unless sediment and rock are regularly removed (Figure 20).

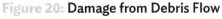

Figure 20: **Damage from Debris Flow**

Source: Study team.

Countermeasures

Although there were few cases of road damage from debris flow, blocked culverts from smaller debris flows were noted.

An effective countermeasure is the debris flow protection installed on National Road A01 near Dili (Figure 21). This solution allows sediment to pass through while large boulders and timbers are caught by a screen installed at the inlet side. However, there is no access for heavy machinery to remove boulders at the inlet side. Providing access would facilitate maintenance efforts.

Figure 21: **Existing Countermeasure for Debris Flow**

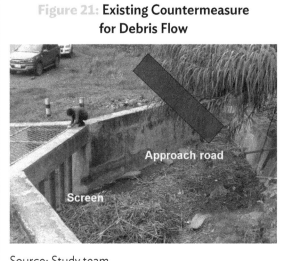

Source: Study team.

Culvert and Ditch

Damage

Rainfall has led to sediment deposits in the ditch due to a collapse on the mountainside, and blockage of the ditch caused water to flow across the road surface over the shoulder on the valley side. As a result, the shoulder on the valley side was eroded, leading to the collapse of both the fill and the retaining wall.

Road damage caused by road ditches and culverts is due to insufficient capacity of the ditches and culverts to handle the received rainfall. In addition, poor maintenance, such as failing to remove sediment from ditches and culverts and not repairing damaged ditches, also contributes to the damage (Figure 22).

Figure 22: **Damage from Culvert and Ditch**

Source: Study team.

Countermeasures

Interviews with local residents revealed that many cases of road damage from rainfall could be related to the recent climate change effects. For future climate change adaptation measures for drainage facilities like culverts and ditches, the following are crucial:

(i)   **Performing flow calculations in response to climate change.** For flow rate calculations for culverts and ditches in response to future climate change, refer to section 2.2 (Impact of Climate Change on the Road Sector in Timor-Leste) in this report.

(ii) **Designing culvert inlets and outlets to manage rainfall and rainfall pressure.** Many fill failures result from ground erosion due to rainfall and hydraulic pressure, in addition to the collapse of the culvert outlet. Countermeasures for these issues are depicted in Figure 23 and Figure 24.

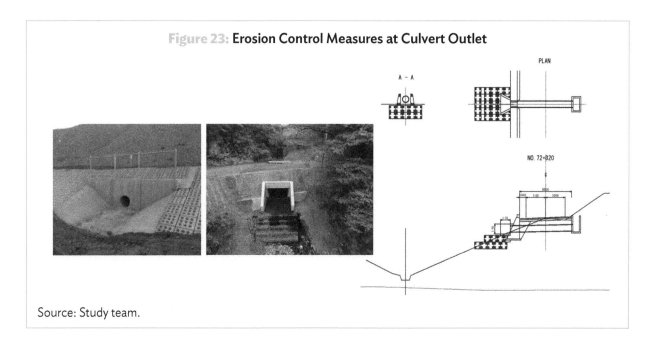

Figure 23: **Erosion Control Measures at Culvert Outlet**

Source: Study team.

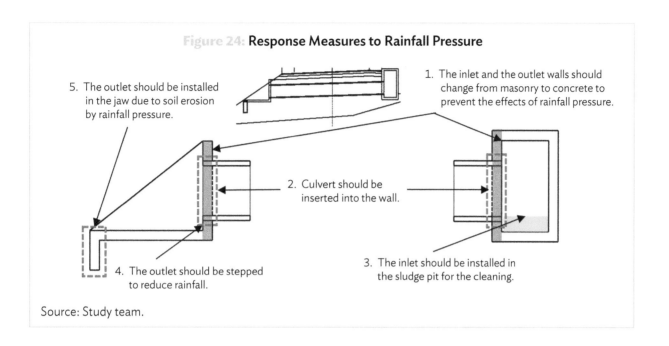

Figure 24: Response Measures to Rainfall Pressure

5. The outlet should be installed in the jaw due to soil erosion by rainfall pressure.

1. The inlet and the outlet walls should change from masonry to concrete to prevent the effects of rainfall pressure.

2. Culvert should be inserted into the wall.

4. The outlet should be stepped to reduce rainfall.

3. The inlet should be installed in the sludge pit for the cleaning.

Source: Study team.

Designing Culvert and Ditch with Maintenance Considerations

In Timor-Leste, culverts for drains are cleaned manually. The minimum diameter for culverts should be φ 1,500 mm. Figure 25(a) illustrates the rationale behind the minimum diameter requirement. The height of a kneeling person is approximately 900 mm, making it challenging to clean inside smaller-diameter culverts. On the other hand, Figure 25(b) demonstrates how a culvert with a height of 1,500 mm allows for easier manual cleaning. Thus, the minimum culvert diameter is also recommended to be 1,500 mm, as described in "(iii) Evaluation of Applicable Box Culvert Size under Historical and Future Climate Scenarios" in the section on "Engineering Design Considering Future Climate Change" under section 2.2 (Impact of Climate Change on the Road Sector in Timor-Leste).

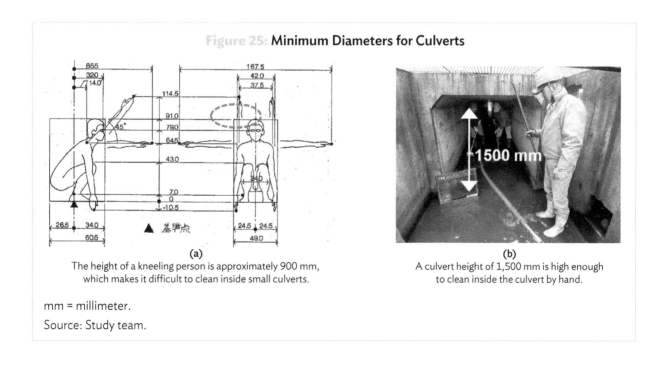

Figure 25: Minimum Diameters for Culverts

(a)
The height of a kneeling person is approximately 900 mm, which makes it difficult to clean inside small culverts.

(b)
A culvert height of 1,500 mm is high enough to clean inside the culvert by hand.

mm = millimeter.

Source: Study team.

Figure 26: **Cleaning Ditches with a Small Excavator**

mm = millimeter.
Source: Study team.

The minimum width for culvert trenches should be at least 450 mm, considering the bucket size of a small hydraulic excavator, to enable mechanized cleaning of sediment deposits (Figure 26).

Resilient Road Cross Section for Climate Change

For road improvement projects in areas with high risk of slope failure, it is proposed to minimize cut slope and/or fill slope by relaxing national standards[9] and adjusting road widths to reduce the risk of road damage. In the immediate future, when traffic volume is low, road improvements will be made at reduced widths. As traffic volume increases in the future, road improvements will be made in accordance with national standards. For example, existing road widths, one-lane road widths, and 1.5-lane road widths shall be considered adjusted road widths (Figure 27). In identifying high-risk road sections, digital elevation model data, topographic data acquired by drones, and GIS analysis should be effectively utilized.

Responding to Future Sea-Level Rise

This study focuses on the impact of heavy rains induced by climate change. In this section, the impact of the future sea-level rise is examined using the National Road A08 along the southern coast as an example. IPCC AR6 predicts a sea-level rise of 0.22 m by 2050 and 0.58 m by 2100 under the +2°C rise scenario near the Uatu Carbau–Uatolari section on National Road A08.

The National Astronomical Observatory (NAO).99b tidal prediction system indicates that the highest astronomical tide level in this area from 2023 to 2099 will be 1.36 m.[10] Furthermore, considering the water-level rise during storm surges, areas approximately 2–3 m above sea level are at risk of inundation, as shown in Map 2.

---

9   Government of Timor-Leste, Ministry of Infrastructure. 2010. *Road Geometric Design Standards.* Dili.

10   NAO.99b Tidal Prediction System. https://www.miz.nao.ac.jp/staffs/nao99/index_En.html.

Figure 27: Example of Narrow Road Widths

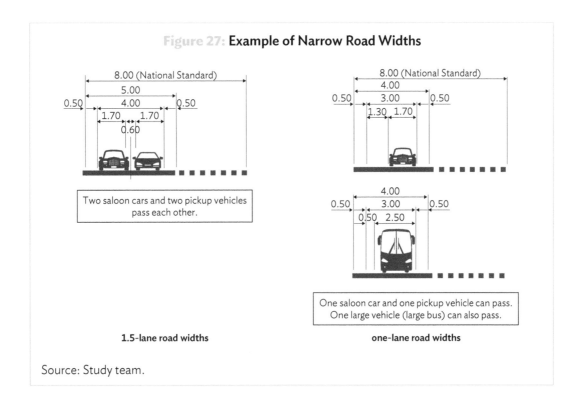

1.5-lane road widths

one-lane road widths

Source: Study team.

Map 2: Potential Inundation Risk Areas (Red Points) Due to Sea-Level Rise at the Uatu Carbau–Uatolari Section on National Road A08

Map data: Google, Image © 2024 Airbus, Image © 2024 TerraMetrics, Data Scripps Institution of Oceanography (SIO), National Oceanic and Atmospheric Administration (NOAA), United States (US) Navy, National Geospatial-Intelligence Agency (NGA), General Bathymetric Chart of the Oceans (GEBCO), Image © 2024 Centre National d'Études Spatiales (CNES)/Airbus.

Source: Study team.

Such areas are at risk of damage not just from rising sea levels but also from high waves and overtopping waves. Therefore, the following wave overtopping measures are necessary:

(i)   linear protection measures such as the installation of seawalls, wave-dissipating blocks, etc.;

(ii)   surface protection measures that combine offshore breakwaters, artificial reefs, beach nourishment, etc.; and

(iii) the installation of coastal embankment.

However, it is crucial to ensure these measures do not adversely affect environmental safeguards. For example, specific sea areas may be within or bordering an environmentally protected area. Balancing the risk of climate impact with environmental safeguards requirements is a critical challenge for engineers and policymakers in road alignment design.

Community-Based Climate Adaptation Measures

Alongside the climate adaptation measures detailed in the previous sections, community participation in these measures is crucial. The study team conducted a case study on a section of National Road A08 where a pilot program for community participation would be applicable.

Damage

Erosion induced by heavy rainfall gradually alters the geometry of both natural and artificial slopes with erodible soil, leading to slope failure along National Road A08. Specific topographic risks along this road include gullying, shallow slumps or planar slips, and bare soil on embankments and cut-face slopes.

Countermeasures

Bioengineering, particularly the use of vegetation on slopes or embankments, offers an alternative solution for slope protection and pollution reduction. Vegetation is an environmentally friendly alternative for ecological restoration and slope stability against rainfall and floods by increasing soil strength through plant roots.

Vetiver grass has been selected for vegetation for its deep root system, reaching 3–4 m, and its resilience to extreme weather conditions.

Vetiver grass bioengineering solution also yields several socioeconomic benefits, including

- job creation for communities, especially women;
- opportunities for green business (e.g., handicrafts) for women; and
- entrepreneurship opportunities in developing Vetiver nurseries and other small and medium-sized enterprises.

A key advantage of Vetiver grass planting is income generation through community women's engagement. Community ownership is essential for the pilot project's success.

A community contract system, coordinated to manage labor-intensive planting work, should be established. An organized group can be mindful of the gender division of labor, accounting for the physical strength, skills, and socioeconomic status of landless laborers or sharecroppers, people with disability, and those with less income or fewer assets.

This study has proposed two bioengineering project sites for embankment and slope erosion protection at Cacavei village in Lautem municipality.

In addition to bioengineering, routine maintenance by the community will foster job creation and economic benefits and encourage maintaining the road network, as summarized in Table 4.

Table 4: **Routine Maintenance by the Community**

Type	Maintenance Description	Contractor	Contract Period	Maintenance Road Coverage
Routine maintenance by the community	Minor works, e.g., trimming and greening, cleaning drains and pipe culverts, removing rocks and fallen trees, and preventing minor landslides	Community contract system set up with community groups under a coordinator to carry out maintenance work	Yearly contract, at least twice a year, before and during the rainy season	Road length in the community contract area

Source: Study team.

2.5 | Damage to Bridges and Countermeasures

Hydraulic studies are essential for guidelines in bridge design over the river (Figure 28).[11] Bridge design over rivers must consider hydraulic phenomena such as rising water, Karman vortices, and lateral flow. It should also prevent significant riverbed fluctuations near bridge piers and avoid proximity to existing structures or past embankment breaches. Therefore, basic guidelines for river bridge design include ensuring clearance exceeds the designed high water level, avoiding turbulent areas, and steering perpendicular to the flow, among others.

Flood Damage—Irabere Bridge

Flood damage at bridges, such as at Irabere Bridge, often stems from scour and washout of approach roads.

Damage

The revetment protecting the abutment on the right bank of Irabere Bridge has been damaged and washed out, with the approach road behind the abutment also affected. The foundation of the abutment was exposed due to the scouring of the approach road. One H-shaped pile (30 cm x 30 cm), which served as the foundation, was broken by the impact of the spilled concrete revetment. In addition, the foundations of the piers experienced scouring (Figure 29).

Due to the exposure and rupture of the H-shaped steel foundation, the right abutment has already lost its ability to withstand design loads. The use of H-shaped steel piles in the abutment foundations is not suitable for conditions prone to scouring conditions. Continued use with reinforcement would make it difficult to ensure the bearing capacity of the foundations. Therefore, the existing abutments should be replaced with new abutments or piers constructed outside the current locations.

---

[11] Japan Institute of Construction Engineering. 2009. Planning Guidance for Bridges Crossing Rivers (draft).

Figure 28: Basic Guidelines for River Bridge Design

Hydraulic phenomena caused by bridge (pier/abutment):	Critical factors to consider regarding hydraulic phenomena:	Basic guideline for river bridge design to adhere to:
• Rising water levels due to a decrease in sediment in the river • Occurrence of downward flow under the bridge piers • Formation of horseshoe vortices[a] • Splashing of water surfaces • Increase in flow velocity from lateral streams • Generation of Karman vortices[b] • Development of shear vortices[c] • Formation of shock waves[d]	• Evaluate the impact on embankments due to increased flow velocity from lateral streams. • Consider local scouring around bridge piers. • Account for long-term fluctuations in the riverbed around bridge piers. • Anticipate rises in water level upstream.	• Ensure that the bridge's clearance height exceeds the designed high water level plus the safety margin. • Avoid areas with changing flow conditions. • Avoid sections of the riverbed with significant fluctuations. • Design the bridge to be perpendicular to the flow direction. • Maintain a safe distance from existing structures. • Steer clear of locations where the river embankment has previously been breached.

Notes:

[a] Vortices formed when water flow abruptly changes direction or encounters obstacles.

[b] Vortices formed behind bridge piers due to a decrease in flow velocity.

[c] Vortices occuring after passing bridge piers due to horizontal flow velocity changes, creating rotational forces horizontally.

[d] Waves generated by impacting the front face of bridge piers and spreading downstream.

Source: Study team.

Figure 29: Deformation of Gabion Wall

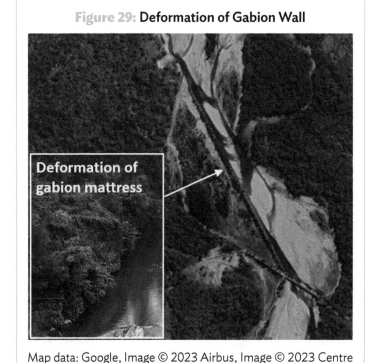

Map data: Google, Image © 2023 Airbus, Image © 2023 Centre National d'Études Spatiales (CNES)/Airbus.

Source: Study team.

The abutment, displaced due to the washout and loss of back soil, moved toward the rear, a situation exacerbated by the loss of one foundation pile and reduced horizontal resistance.

The girder shifted 2 cm upstream and 5 cm downstream. The joint spacing in the normal section is approximately 3 cm, and this displacement of the girder may have increased the horizontal force on the rubber bearings.

The piers are receiving river flow from the front when they should receive it from the sides, and the foundations of the piers are exposed, indicating that the scour is progressing.

In addition to the washout of the approach road to the bridge, the gabion wall has been deformed due to the effects of the river's narrower width and faster velocity.

Back of Irabere Bridge abutment. Embankment of an approach road was eroded and then a bridge abutment and its foundation piles are exposed.

Rupture of abutment foundation piles of Irabere Bridge. The breakage in the foundation piles demonstrates the structural vulnerabilities faced by the bridge, signaling the essential need for foundation reinforcement or redesign.

Pier foundation of Irabere Bridge being scoured. The flow is disrupted around a pier. Due to the effects of turbulent flow, riverbed is locally scoured.

Countermeasures

Construction of a Relief Bridge with Tree Planting

The installation of a relief bridge (box or bridge), as illustrated in Figure 30 and Figure 31, should be considered at the rear of the abutment. The choice between a bridge or a box culvert should be based on a comprehensive evaluation of constructability and economic efficiency. Detailed surveying and geological investigation should be conducted. The general procedures for constructing a relief bridge are the following:

(1) Support the main girder with a temporary bearing and check its condition. If excessive displacement is detected, reposition the main girder using a jack. Then, remove the existing abutment and install new foundation piles on both sides.

(2) Demolish the existing abutments, cut the existing piles, and install new foundation piles on both sides of the abutments.

(3) Construct new pier abutments on the foundation piles.

(4) Complete a relief bridge on the approach that is continuous with the pier abutments.

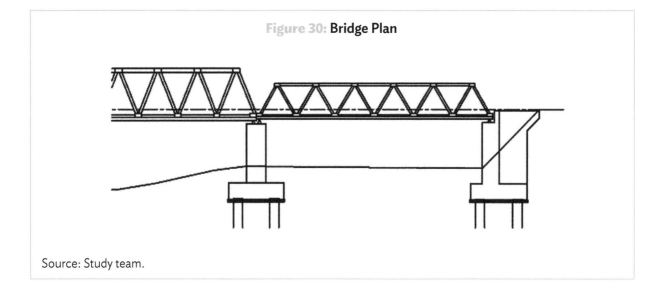

Figure 30: **Bridge Plan**

Source: Study team.

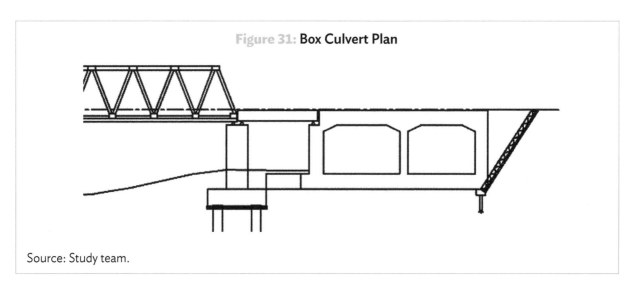

Figure 31: **Box Culvert Plan**

Source: Study team.

Additionally, tree planting at the opening between the abutment on the right bank and the gabion wall is advised to protect the approach road from the direct impact of flood flow (Figure 32). Two-dimensional flow simulation shows that the velocity at the approach road decreases by 0.65 meters per second (m/s) with tree planting, effectively preventing scouring.

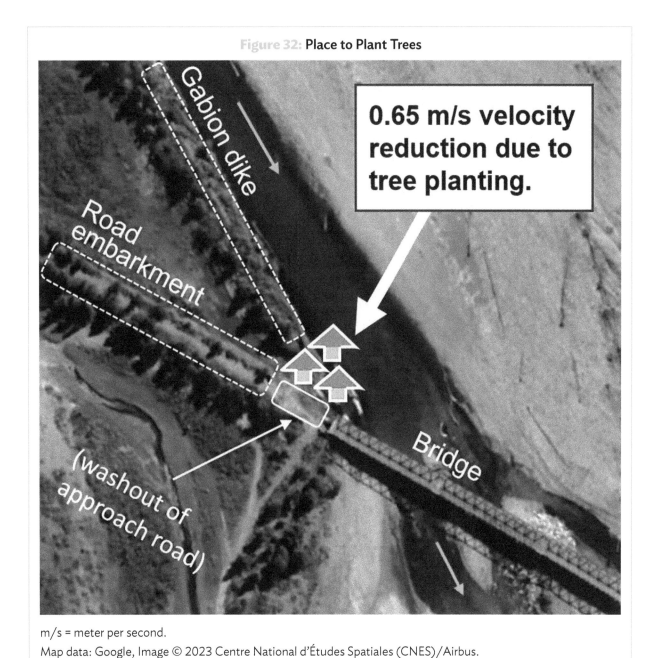

Figure 32: **Place to Plant Trees**

m/s = meter per second.
Map data: Google, Image © 2023 Centre National d'Études Spatiales (CNES)/Airbus.
Source: Study team.

Installation of Rooting Works (Bedding Blocks and Steel Sheet Pile Closure) Around the Piers

The piers on the right bank are facing direct water flow, leading to the scouring of their foundations. These foundations need to be protected by root-consolidation works such as bedding blocks (Figure 33). The type of root-consolidation work should be determined after a thorough analysis of river flow conditions.

Installation of Groins in the Front of the Gabion Wall

Groins should be installed to prevent the collapse of the gabion wall due to increased water velocity (Figure 34).

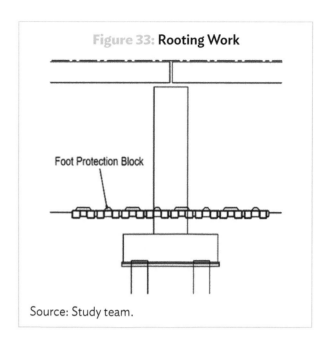

Figure 33: **Rooting Work**

Foot Protection Block

Source: Study team.

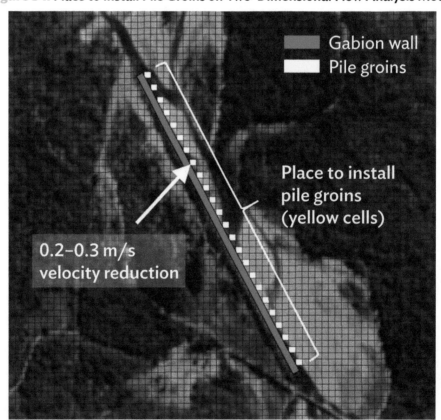

Figure 34: **Place to Install Pile Groins on Two-Dimensional Flow Analysis Model**

Gabion wall
Pile groins

Place to install pile groins (yellow cells)

0.2–0.3 m/s velocity reduction

m/s = meter per second.
Map data: Google, Image © 2023 Centre National d'Études Spatiales (CNES)/Airbus.
Source: Study team.

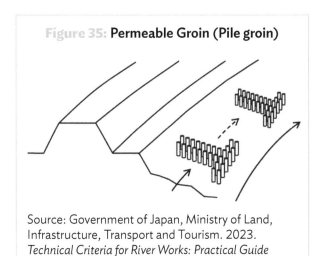

Figure 35: Permeable Groin (Pile groin)

Source: Government of Japan, Ministry of Land,
Infrastructure, Transport and Tourism. 2023.
*Technical Criteria for River Works: Practical Guide
for Design*. Tokyo.

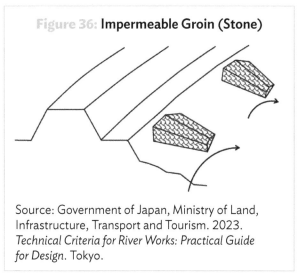

Figure 36: Impermeable Groin (Stone)

Source: Government of Japan, Ministry of Land,
Infrastructure, Transport and Tourism. 2023.
*Technical Criteria for River Works: Practical Guide
for Design*. Tokyo.

There are two structural types of groins: (i) permeable groins, effective in reducing velocity and sediment deposition (Figure 35); and (ii) impermeable groins, which direct the flow to the center of the river channel (Figure 36). Two-dimensional flow simulations indicate that permeable groins decrease the velocity at the front of the gabion wall by 0.2–0.3 m/s during peak flow times. Installing groins in front of the gabion wall is expected to function as a roughness factor, reducing velocity and preventing scour with sediment deposition.

Heavy Sedimentation Under the Welolo Bridge

The Welolo Bridge has sustained damage due to sediment accumulation, leading to insufficient water flow at the cross sections.

Damage

Sediment from upstream has significantly accumulated on the riverbed below the Welolo Bridge girder. In July 2023, a large amount of driftwood from upstream was trapped by the bridge girders. A strong flood flow could displace the main girder, risking bridge failure. In addition, changes in the river's course have caused water from directly upstream of the bridge to flow toward the road, impeding traffic and causing progressive scouring of the slope of the approach road. Despite these issues, the bridge and its slabs were in good condition, showing no signs of corrosion or missing bolts.

River Engineering Perspective

Floodwater rose due to riverbed aggradation and low clearance (60–80 cm) under the bridge, leading to overtopping on the right riverbank (Figure 37). Overflowed water ran onto National Road A07, about 1 km to the west, altering its flow southward off the road before sinking into the ground and disappearing (Figure 38).

Accumulation of driftwood at Welolo Bridge. Rising riverbeds due to sediment deposition and the accumulation of driftwood pose a significant risk to flood inundation and bridge stability.

River flow toward the road at Welolo Bridge. Altered river flow directs water toward the road, disrupting traffic and progressively scouring the approach road's slope.

Approach road washed out at Welolo Bridge. The road leading to the bridge has been turned into a river and is impassable due to the change in the river channel.

Figure 37: Riverbed Aggradation and Overtopping

River flow is divided into two ways, (i) original flow crossing Welolo bridge, and (ii) overflow directed to AO7 Road.

Clearance under the bridge is 60–80 cm

cm = centimeter.
Source: Study team.

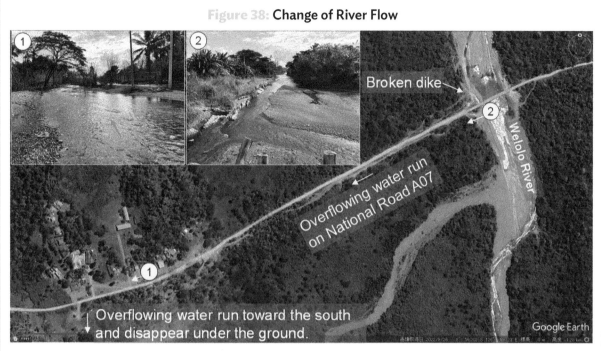

Figure 38: Change of River Flow

Broken dike

Welolo River

Overflowing water run on National Road A07

Overflowing water run toward the south and disappear under the ground.

Google Earth

Map data: Google, Image © 2023 Airbus.
Source: Study team.

Countermeasures for Restoration

Rerouting National Road A07 is advisable due to difficulties in maintaining the original flow through the bridge, exacerbated by upstream sediment buildup on the riverbed and scouring of the access road.

To identify an optimal bypass route considering probable flood areas, the study team used a two-dimensional flood simulation. The simulation suggests a high possibility of flood expansion south from the downstream end of the vanishing river, an area historically part of the stream now obscured by sediment deposition. Shifting the road route to less flood-prone north/south sides ensures a passable route. Choosing the optimal solution among three options (Route A, B, and C), shown in Figure 39, requires detailed topographic surveying (to secure specific routes by filling in flooded areas) and records of past flood extents.

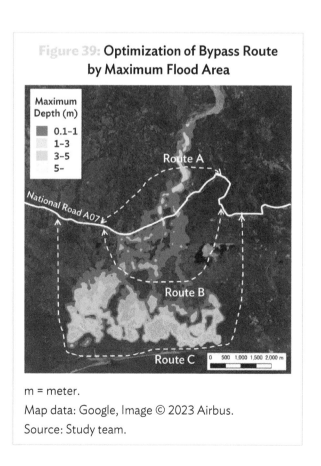

Figure 39: Optimization of Bypass Route by Maximum Flood Area

Maximum Depth (m)
0.1–1
1–3
3–5
5–

Route A

National Road A07

Route B

Route C

0 500 1,000 1,500 2,000 m

m = meter.
Map data: Google, Image © 2023 Airbus.
Source: Study team.

Low-Water Bridge Based on Risk Tolerance

Background

Constructing a low-water bridge is a viable solution for crossing rivers with low traffic volumes and a high risk of bridge damage. A low-water bridge, a low-elevation roadway over a river, remains dry above the water during low flow but submerges during floods. With increased road traffic, transitioning to a conventional bridge for stable traffic flow becomes essential. Designing a low-water bridge without handrails prevents obstruction by driftwood or debris during floods.

Low-water bridge during dry season. Low-water bridges are a viable option where traffic volumes are low and bridges are susceptible to damage during flooding.

Low-water bridge in Timor-Leste. This type of low-water bridge is passable even during the rainy season, except during floods.

Condition

Ensuring a low-water bridge does not exacerbate flood damage requires careful planning of an appropriate bridge height by assessing river water-level fluctuations.

The construction of a low-water bridge must consider the surrounding living environment to prevent potential river damming during floods. In addition, installing a low-water bridge in areas prone to significant soil and sand accumulation necessitates plans to manage and mitigate further accumulation.

Periodical monitoring for bridge management generally falls under three main categories.[12]

- **Bridge piers.** Conduct pre-flood season visual inspections for embankment cracks near bridge piers, undertaking detailed investigations as needed and appropriate measures such as repairs.

- **Bridge abutments**. Monitor scour shapes (maximum depth and extent) around bridge abutments, taking corrective actions for river management issues identified.

- **Approaching roads.** Promptly address pavement cracks in the approach roads to the bridge to prevent water channel formation, with road managers implementing swift corrective actions.

Understanding the overall sediment balance upstream and downstream and the changes in sediment supply to the bridge components are necessary for long-term monitoring.

---

[12] Ministry of Land, Infrastructure, Transport and Tourism. 2011. The Japanese Ministry of Land, Infrastructure, Transport and Tourism Technical Criteria for River Works: Guide for Maintenance/Management (in Japanese). ijikanri_honbun.pdf (mlit.go.jp).

2.6 | Capacity Development

Field Training

Capacity development is a key pillar of this study. The team capitalized on various opportunities for the capacity development of government engineers. Activities included joint field surveys with the Ministry of Public Works (MPW) engineers, periodic technical meetings, field workshops (study site tour), and training in using the newly procured equipment.

The field workshops and equipment utilization training are detailed below.

Field Workshops (Study Site Tours)

In addition to regular field surveys, two field workshops (study site tours) were conducted for engineers from the Directorate General of Roads, Bridges, Prevention and Flood Control (DGRBPFC) and the Project Management Unit of the MPW, as well as engineers from the National Development Agency (ADN) and the Ministry of Planning and Territory.

These workshops aimed to strengthen the capacity of government engineers in assessing and identifying road damage causes and considering climate change adaptation measures on site (Table 5).

Table 5: Field Workshops

Training	Major Activities	Date	Participants
First field workshop at KM72 on Road A09 and KM103 on Road A01	• Observation of road damage caused by fill slope failure on-site • Consideration of appropriate solutions to prevent fill slope failure by applying bench cuts and compaction, appropriate design of the retaining wall and drainage outlets, and quality control by using a checklist for construction • Safety measures at construction sites	15 August 2023	25 engineers from MPW and ADN
Technical briefing for the second field workshop	• A technical briefing was held prior to the second field workshop to enhance the participants' on-site understanding.	15 September 2023	30 engineers from MPW
Second field workshop at KM92 on Road A09	• Confirmation of road damage and changes in the surrounding topography due to landslides from a comprehensive perspective on-site • Confirmation and explanation of the geotechnical investigation results • Observation of groundwater levels • Demonstration of geoelectrical resistivity survey and topographic survey using a drone with LiDAR	18 September 2023	31 engineers from MPW

ADN = National Development Agency, LiDAR = light detection and ranging, MPW = Ministry of Public Works.
Source: Study team.

First field workshop on National Road A09.
The field workshop was conducted to strengthen the capacity of government engineers to assess and identify the causes of road damage in the field.

Technical briefing for the second field workshop.
A technical briefing was held prior to the second field workshop to help participants gain a better understanding of the field.

Second field workshop on National Road A09.
Participants closely examined the results of geotechnical investigations and groundwater level observations on-site.

Technical Training

As outlined in "Use of Innovative Technologies" under section 2.6 (Capacity Development) in this knowledge product, this study introduced new technologies, including drones with light detection and ranging (LiDAR) sensors, 3D mapping software, and geoelectrical resistivity equipment. To ensure sustainable and effective usage, training sessions on operating these tools were conducted for MPW engineers (Table 6).

In addition, a training course was provided for officers responsible for rainfall data at relevant organizations, focusing on how to utilize the satellite-observed rainfall data produced and distributed by the Japan Aerospace Exploration Agency (JAXA).

Table 6: Technical Training

Training	Description	Date	Participants
Training on geoelectrical resistivity equipment by the manufacturer	Three MPW engineers received training on using the geoelectrical resistivity equipment in Bandung, Indonesia.	22–23 August 2023	3 engineers from MPW
Training on geoelectrical resistivity equipment for MPW engineers	Three MPW engineers who received the above training conducted the training for other MPW engineers on-site.	22 September 2023	18 engineers from MPW
Training on utilization of drone with LiDAR sensor	The study team conducted training on using the drone with LiDAR on-site.	28–29 September 2023	14 engineers from MPW
Training on utilization of satellite-observed rainfall data	The study team conducted training on utilizing satellite-observed rainfall data.	5–15 December 2023	23 engineers from MPW, MPS, ADN, DNMG, and UNTL

ADN = National Development Agency, DNMG = National Directorate of Meteorology and Geophysics, LiDAR = light detection and ranging, MPS = Major Projects Secretariat, MPW = Ministry of Public Works, UNTL = National University of Timor-Leste (Universidade Nacional Timor Lorosa'e).
Source: Study team.

Use of Innovative Technologies

Timor-Leste's geographical location makes it highly vulnerable to climate change impacts, including extreme weather events, changing precipitation patterns, rising sea levels, and increasing temperatures. Utilizing innovative technologies is crucial for effectively addressing these challenges in the road sector, enhancing the capacity of government engineers in road administration.

Remote Sensing, Geographic Information Systems, and Global Navigation Satellite System

These technologies provide valuable data for climate monitoring and analysis. Satellite and drone imagery, geographic information system (GIS), and global navigation satellite system enable the assessment of vulnerable areas, prediction of climate-related risks, and effective road infrastructure planning.

Training on geoelectrical resistivity equipment in Bandung, Indonesia. An engineer demonstrates the equipment's operation on a side street as colleagues observe, focusing on mastering the technology for field application.

Training on geoelectrical resistivity equipment at KM92 on National Road A09. A hands-on session where participants engage with cutting-edge technology. This will enhance their understanding and skills in geoelectrical analysis.

Training on drone with LiDAR on National Road A09. Participants learn aerial surveying techniques essential for advanced road analysis together with the expert from the National University of Timor-Leste.

Training on utilization of satellite-observed rainfall data. Participants enthusiastically learned from Japanese experts how to acquire satellite-observed rainfall and use it for various analyses.

Drone with LiDAR

This study introduced a drone equipped with LiDAR, offering detailed and accurate topographic data with significant advantages:

- **High-resolution topographic mapping.** The drone enables the creation of high-resolution digital elevation models, providing insights into terrain topography and ground movement morphology. This information is crucial for civil engineering projects such as roads, bridges, rivers, and dams.
- **Surface-change detection.** The drone's capability for repeated scans aids in the early detection of surface changes, which is critical for monitoring dynamic geological processes like landslides and erosion.
- **Vegetation and land cover mapping.** With its ability to penetrate vegetation, the drone reveals detailed information on land cover and vegetation structure, which is useful in environmental impact studies and ecosystem management.
- **Geological risk assessment.** It identifies geological faults, terrain instabilities, and other geological features of interest for assessing geological risks.
- **Road planning and maintenance.** The drone contributes to road planning by providing accurate data for infrastructure design and road maintenance management.

Geological and Geotechnical Engineering

Geological and geotechnical engineering are pivotal in implementing climate change adaptation measures, particularly in mitigating the impacts of climate change on infrastructure and the natural environment.

Geoelectrical Resistivity Equipment

The geoelectric resistivity equipment procured under this study is expected to provide the following benefits in road planning:

- **Mapping of geological structures.** Electrical resistivity helps map various geological layers by detecting variations in subsoil resistivity, crucial to understanding stratigraphy and groundwater distribution.
- **Location of aquifers and groundwater.** The technique is instrumental in identifying aquifers and mapping groundwater distribution, which is essential for assessing groundwater's role in ground instability and water resources management.
- **Assessment of subsurface structures.** It is used to evaluate slope stability, identify underground caves, and characterize construction materials.
- **Environmental monitoring.** Electrical resistivity is applied in environmental studies to monitor changes in groundwater distribution and identify potential environmental impacts.

Use of Satellite-Observed Rainfall Data

Data on past short-term rainfall intensity (hourly rainfall) are essential for assessing the impact of climate change on infrastructure damage. In Timor-Leste, only daily rainfall is observed, with limited historical records available. The study team has projected rainfall changes due to climate change in Timor-Leste by applying satellite-observed rainfall data (GSMaP) from JAXA, available hourly since 1998. These data are valuable not only for road infrastructure planning but also for meteorology, disaster prevention, climate monitoring, agricultural monitoring, and water resources management. Training on the use of satellite-observed rainfall data was provided to government officials responsible for rainfall data management.

Geographic Information Systems Mapping
for Climate Change Adaptation

Target Road Section and Workflow

The study team selected a target road section from Lospalos to Iliomar on National Road A08 for GIS mapping of climate change risks. This section, being at a relatively higher altitude than other sections on National Road A08, is considered at high risk for slope disasters due to climate change. GIS is a suitable tool for mapping such wide-ranging risks.

Extraction of Areas with High Risk of Slope Failure

A mountainous region spreads out in the southern part of the section. Using digital elevation model data from the Ministry of Planning and Territory, areas with slopes of 30–35 degrees (yellow in Map 3) and larger than 35 degrees (red in Map 3) were identified through GIS as having high slope failure risks, potentially impacting National Road A08. These areas require careful consideration from the start of the road design phase in future projects.

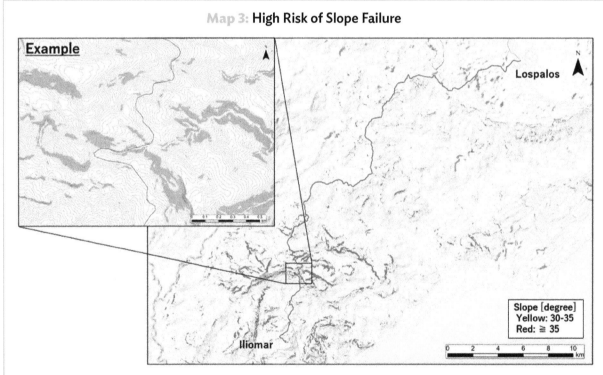

Map 3: High Risk of Slope Failure

Map data: Environmental Systems Research Institute (Esri), HERE, Garmin, Intermap, increment P Corp., General Bathymetric Chart of the Oceans (GEBCO), United States Geological Survey (USGS), Food and Agriculture Organization of the United Nations (FAO), National Park Service (NPS), Natural Resources Canada (NRCAN), GeoBase, Institut National de l'Information Géographique et Forestière (IGN), Kadaster NL, Ordnance Survey, Esri Japan, Ministry of Economy, Trade and Industry, Japan (METI), Esri China (Hong Kong, China), ©OpenStreetMap contributors, and the Geographic Information System (GIS) User Community.

Source: Study team.

Hydrological Analysis and Fieldwork

The hydrological conditions in this area were analyzed using GIS, leading to the creation of a pseudo stream network (Figure 40) and the extraction of intersections with the road. The study team collaborated with the GIS section at DGRBPFC to discuss the results and carried out field surveys at each intersection to observe the presence or absence of culverts and assess their condition. A drone was employed to capture images of areas inaccessible to people. The data from the field surveys, including observations and photographs of the culverts, were integrated into GIS and compiled. This database, combined with the extraction results indicating a high risk of slope failure, can be effectively used for the early stages of road design in future projects. These mapping processes are set to provide support for ESTRADA, the Road Asset Management system.

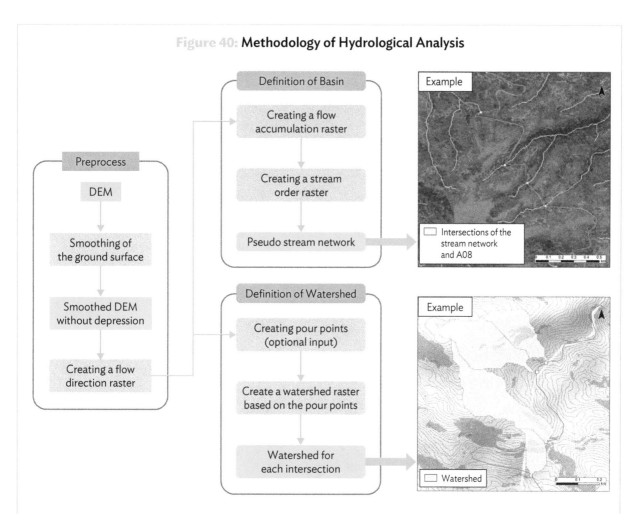

Figure 40: **Methodology of Hydrological Analysis**

DEM = digital elevation model.

Map data: Above: Environmental Systems Research Institute (Esri), Maxar, Earthstar Geographics, and the Geographic Information System (GIS) User Community.

Below: Esri, HERE, Garmin, Intermap, increment P Corp., General Bathymetric Chart of the Oceans (GEBCO), United States Geological Survey (USGS), Food and Agriculture Organization of the United Nations (FAO), National Park Service (NPS), Natural Resources Canada (NRCAN), GeoBase, National Geographic Institute, France (IGN), Kadaster NL, Ordnance Survey, Esri Japan, Ministry of Economy, Trade, and Industry, Japan (METI), Esri China (Hong Kong, China), ©OpenStreetMap contributors, and the GIS User Community.

Source: Study team.

3 IMPORTANT POINTS FOR FUTURE ROAD DEVELOPMENT

This study has addressed assessments and proposals for climate change adaptation measures. This chapter outlines five key considerations for implementing these measures in future road development in Timor-Leste.

3.1 | Climate Adaptation Measures Are Needed for All Project Cycles

At the outset, this report posed a critical question: why are roads frequently damaged only a few years after construction? As discussed in previous chapters, several factors contribute to this issue in Timor-Leste: (i) the mismatch between current road designs and the recent and future severe climate conditions, (ii) weak quality control for climate adaptation in road construction, and (iii) lack of maintenance for sustaining the climate resilience of road assets. Thus, climate adaptation measures should be integrated into all three project cycles—design, construction, and maintenance, as indicated in Figure 41.

Figure 41: Project Cycles and Climate Adaptation Measures

Design	Construction	Maintenance
• Supplement/amend standard specifications with climate change consideration	• Quality control as per specifications, guidelines and checklists, which are already with the Employer	• Maintenance budgeting under Infrastructure Fund and/or Line Ministry Budget
• Utilize more climate-resilient engineering solutions	• Shop drawing and cost amendment for climate-resilient solutions as per site-specific situations (Employer and ADN shall accept necessary cost increase when justified)	• Pool of emergency budget
• Design review by Employer as per the updated standards and guidelines		• More small equipment preparation on site
• Alignment option via risk-based approach with relaxed standards		• Community participation in drainage cleaning and planting for slope protection

ADN = National Development Agency.
Source: Study team.

In the **design** phase, the standard technical specification needs to be supplemented or amended based on recent findings, such as determining the appropriate drainage size to accommodate climate changes, as discussed in section 2.2 (Impact of Climate Change on the Road Sector in Timor-Leste). This study introduced viable climate-resilient engineering solutions, which the Employer should consider during the design review. A risk-based approach is also recommended for the design stage. Furthermore, the government should update the national design standards to reflect climate change, highlighting practical parameters and engineering solutions. These findings will be incorporated into the detailed engineering design for damage-rectification works. ADB will keep seeking opportunities to support the government in updating national standards.

In the **construction** phase, the Employer should enforce stricter quality control. There may be cases where adjustments to original drawings and costs are warranted and should be approved by the Employer (and the National Development Agency [ADN] if applicable) for climate-resilient solutions at the construction stage.

The **maintenance** phase requires recurrent and periodic maintenance based on a road maintenance plan. Frequent inspections of drainage and road surfaces are necessary, especially for roads in Timor-Leste's hilly regions. Introducing small equipment for cleaning ditches, as described in section 2.4 (Culvert and Ditch), is an effective way to improve road maintenance. Encouraging community participation in road maintenance is also beneficial. Maintenance budgets need to be secured under the Infrastructure Fund or the line ministry budget, including a pooled budget for emergency repairs, to cover the rehabilitation of damaged roads and routine maintenance.

3.2 | The Employer Should Be Empowered to Manage Climate Resilience

The Ministry of Public Works (MPW), as the Employer, should use its capacity for design review and quality control of the contractor by employing updated specifications and guidelines with climate change considerations, as well as quality checklists (Figure 42). With the empowerment of the Employer, the ADN should focus more on process audits for internationally financed projects because the current role of the ADN overlaps with the requirement of the International Federation of Consulting Engineers (FIDIC) for the Engineer (supervision consultants).

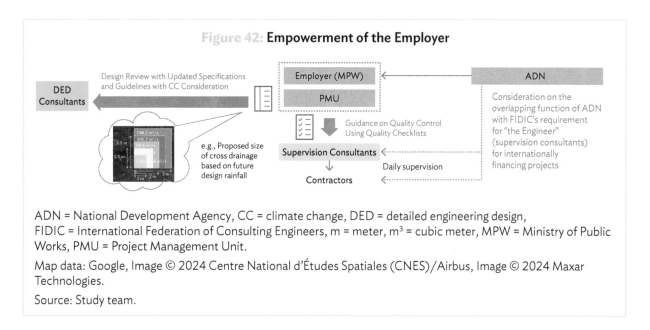

Figure 42: Empowerment of the Employer

ADN = National Development Agency, CC = climate change, DED = detailed engineering design, FIDIC = International Federation of Consulting Engineers, m = meter, m³ = cubic meter, MPW = Ministry of Public Works, PMU = Project Management Unit.

Map data: Google, Image © 2024 Centre National d'Études Spatiales (CNES)/Airbus, Image © 2024 Maxar Technologies.

Source: Study team.

3.3 | Comprehensive Approach Is Recommended for Technical Assessment

Under the comprehensive approach, engineers must adopt a broader view, which means investigating beyond the damaged road section to understand the true cause of damage. This approach requires using innovative technologies such as a drone with light detection and ranging (LiDAR) sensors and traditional methods like geotechnical and field investigations, even in bushland away from the road sections. As analyzed in section 2.4 (Landslide and Cut Slope Failure), stability calculations, safety factor considerations, and topographic and geotechnical surveys of a larger area are crucial. Given that the road network in Timor-Leste often traverses steeply terraced coastal areas and the spine of the island, the Employer should ensure that the design consultancy has sufficient drainage and geotechnical engineers to provide appropriate slope protection measures.

3.4 | Risk-Based Approach Is Suggested to Select Climate Adaptation Measures

This study recommends using geographic information system (GIS) at the design stage to identify sections with high landslide risk (Figure 43). Design measures should be chosen based on three risk policies: avoid risk, mitigate risk, and accept risk. In this assessment, applying a cost–benefit analysis is essential, as opting for an expensive solution without considering the expected benefits is not advisable. For example, in locations with fragile soil, challenging topography, and a high landslide likelihood, but low expected traffic, it might be advisable to avoid cut and fill slopes as much as possible and accept a narrower road width with 1.5 lanes by relaxing the national standard for the particular road section.

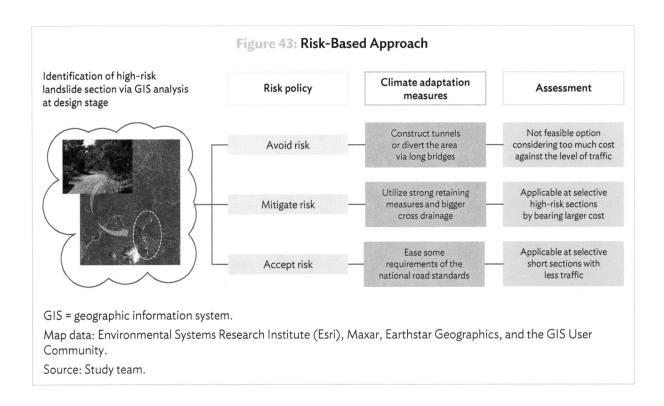

Figure 43: **Risk-Based Approach**

GIS = geographic information system.
Map data: Environmental Systems Research Institute (Esri), Maxar, Earthstar Geographics, and the GIS User Community.
Source: Study team.

3.5 | Community Participation and Perception Are Important

The community is expected to actively engage in climate adaptation measures. As introduced in section 2.4 (Community-Based Climate Adaptation Measures), activities such as planting for slope protection and cleaning roadside ditches can be undertaken with community participation. This approach not only addresses local labor needs but also fosters a sense of ownership among residents for maintaining roads in the provinces. Additionally, raising public awareness of climate adaptation measures is crucial, which can be supported by disseminating information through the media (Figure 44).[13]

Figure 44: Proposed Pilot Community Participation in Bioengineering Slope Protection

CL = center line, m = meter.
Source: Study team.

---

[13] "Towards Climate-Resilient Roads in Timor-Leste." YouTube video, 4:32. Posted by the Asian Development Bank (ADB), 20 October 2023. https://youtu.be/pHvAZaMnVVA. The video is also available in Tetum (local language) on the ADB Timor-Leste Resident Mission's Facebook page: "Halo Estrada Neebé Reziliente Ba Klimátika Iha Timor-Leste." Facebook video, 4:48. Posted by ADB Timor-Leste, 8 November 2023.

Printed in the USA
CPSIA information can be obtained
at www.ICGtesting.com
LVHW060923191124
797022LV00012B/99

* 9 7 8 9 2 9 2 7 0 7 9 2 7 *